600

Beyond Tears

A Story of One Family's Survival of the
1900 Hurricane of Galveston, Texas

KATHLEEN STEELE

authorHOUSE®

AuthorHouse™
1663 Liberty Drive
Bloomington, IN 47403
www.authorhouse.com
Phone: 1 (800) 839-8640

Published by AuthorHouse 03/25/2019

ISBN: 978-1-5462-7070-6 (sc)
ISBN: 978-1-5462-7068-3 (hc)
ISBN: 978-1-5462-7069-0 (e)

Library of Congress Control Number: 2018914211

Print information available on the last page.

Any people depicted in stock imagery provided by Getty Images are models, and such images are being used for illustrative purposes only. Certain stock imagery © Getty Images.

This book is printed on acid-free paper.

Because of the dynamic nature of the Internet, any web addresses or links contained in this book may have changed since publication and may no longer be valid. The views expressed in this work are solely those of the author and do not necessarily reflect the views of the publisher, and the publisher hereby disclaims any responsibility for them.

Dedicated to
George G., Sr. and Lillie Steele
And
All My Grandchildren

And In Loving Memory
To
George G. Steele, II

Chapter 1

1900

She woke up earlier than usual and wondered if she had slept at all. It was nearly impossible to sleep on these hot August nights in this Texas coastal town. Not only was it the heat, but added to her misery was the humidity that draped the town like a wet blanket.

As Rosanna quietly slipped out of bed, she tried to not disturb her husband, James. Her damp nightgown clung to her body. In the darkness of predawn she went over to the dresser and poured some water into the bowl. She pushed up the sleeves of her nightgown and proceeded to wash her face and neck; then she sprinkled some water onto her shoulders and arms. Quickly, she dried herself and changed into her dry day dress. Even if the water had been warm, it refreshed her enough to face the day.

Rosanna walked through the small parlor into the even smaller kitchen, she thought to herself, *I have about as much energy as Elgiva's rag doll and probably look as ragged as it does.* She had not fully regained her strength after the birth of her youngest child, Mary. Rosanna felt this condition was due more to the heat than the new baby. She had five other children who had not taken such a toll on her, or perhaps it was her age. She was now thirty-seven years old. More than likely, it could be a combination of all three; age, new baby, and the unbearable heat.

Her early rising had given a little extra time to get breakfast started and, if she was lucky, have a cup of coffee before Mary would be needing her next morning feeding. The demands of her large family would fill every minute of every hour.

There were the rare times she could actually take a short nap, but that depended on getting her three youngest children to all take a nap at the same time. Getting Roy (four years old) and Albert (two years old) to get in bed for a rest was the easy part, getting them to settle down and be quiet was another matter. But nap time was hours away.

Now the smell of coffee drifted through the house signaling to the other waking family members that the heart of the home was up and making breakfast. A pot of porridge was simmering on the stove. Rosanna was busy slicing some bread and taking an occasional sip of coffee when James entered the kitchen. "How did you sleep?" he asked her as he bent over to give her a kiss on the cheek. He got his cup off the table and went over to the stove to pour himself a cup of coffee. "Need a warm up?"

She was almost too tired to answer him. "No thanks. I'm good." She was a little envious of her husband's ability to sleep through anything. Regardless of what was happening around him, whether it was the weather, a barking dog or a fretful child, James Steele could sleep through it all. Either that or he was a master at 'playing possum'. He was a kind man and did care deeply for his wife and family, but rarely did anything interrupt his sleep.

Rosanna had thought she was destined to be a farmer's wife. In the early years of their marriage James tried his hand at farming. He was raised on a farm and one would think it would come naturally to him, but it didn't. With a desire for an education and the courage to stretch his endeavors into a field no one else in his family had yet attempted, he had gone to college and earned his teaching certificate. It had not been easy. Teaching positions had proved to be almost as unpredictable as farming. Yet, the family's financial struggles did not deter him from pursuing this new career. The farmer's wife was now a teacher's wife. It proved to be the best type of work for him and his growing family. The ability to move to different parts of the country played an important role in the welfare of his family.

Rosanna finished slicing the bread and got up to go check on Earl. She had barely gotten out of her chair, when Earl walked through the doorway, pulling up his suspenders and tucking in his shirt. He joined his parents at the table. As they ate their breakfast he and his father briefly discussed the day's plans.

Even though Earl was only twelve years old, he had an active role in helping with his siblings. His part-time job delivering papers for the Galveston Daily News also helped with the family finances.

It wasn't long before his two younger sisters, Junieta and Elgiva, were at the table, eating their breakfast. Roy and Albert were the last to come shuffling to the kitchen. Roy, being the older of the two, took his role as older brother very seriously, as if it was his sole responsibility. He was so glad when his position as the baby of the family was passed to Albert. The fact he had a baby sister had not yet registered with him. He was totally focused on Albert. With a slight degree of exertion, Roy tried to help Albert climb up to get in his high chair. After the younger brother was finally settled, Roy began to feed his brother.

His father gently stopped him, "Roy, you are a big help to your brother, but he's big enough to feed himself. If you keep doing everything for him, he'll never learn to do for himself."

"But Papa, he's so messy_____"

"And so were you when you were two years old. Neatness comes with age and instruction from your parents."

The subject was closed. Earl knew it and so did Junieta and Elgiva. Roy was the persistent one. "But, Papa, I can help him do better."

"Son, you can be a good example for him. He'll learn. I promise. Now, get to your own breakfast."

The rest of the morning meal was taken in relative quietness until interrupted by Mary's cries for attention. It was now time for her breakfast.

Rosanna got up to go attend to Mary. The two older sisters started to clear the table and stack the dishes in the sink. Roy and Albert continued to eat their breakfast, Roy struggling hard to not help his younger brother. Earl and his father had finished their meal and both left to go do some morning chores before heading to town.

Rosanna returned to the kitchen with baby Mary cradled in her arms. The baby was slowly drifting off for another trip into dreamland, completely satisfied with a full tummy and dry clothing.

A small squabble was brewing between Elgiva and Roy. It seemed she was trying to usurp Roy's authority by starting to help clean Albert's face and take him out of the high chair. Roy did not like this one bit. Rosanna breathed a deep sigh.

"Girls, that's fine. You've helped enough for now. The boys are almost done. I'll finish the dishes. Junieta, here, take the baby to the front porch. I'll be there in a minute. Elgiva, you go with her. Get some fresh air before the day gets any hotter." The girls gladly obeyed their mother's command.

Rosanna cleared the rest of the dishes, washed and dried them. She wiped off the table with a clean soapy rag. Glancing around the kitchen she felt satisfied all was in good order. She called Roy and Albert to come with her and they joined the girls on the front porch. Mary was sound asleep. She didn't even make a slight whimper as Rosanna took her and traded places with Junieta, who promptly took a place on the floor of the porch. Elgiva was waiting for her sister to play a game of Jacks. Albert wanted to join them. He was fascinated by the small bouncing red ball. Roy pulled him away with the promise he had a better game for him to play.

James and Earl walked from the back of the house to join the family, having completed the needed chores. Earl had gathered enough eggs to sell to the local grocer. James had filled the wood box with enough firewood to meet the day's needs, which were few during this hot spell; cooking was kept to a minimum. There was never a day that passed that the stove wasn't needed for something, even if it was just to heat the water to wash the dishes.

James walked up the front steps to say goodby to Rosanna and the rest of his children. Earl waited at the bottom of the steps, saving his energy for his paper route, which required a lot of walking. James never tired of seeing his children happily entertaining themselves. The girls were becoming quite skillful with their game of Jacks, and the boys were busily chasing a butterfly—no net, just using their little hands. He turned his attention to his wife of fourteen years. She was eight years younger than he, but today she showed signs of aging he hadn't noticed before. Rosanna saw the look in his eyes and interpreted its meaning. She knew he was worried about her health. She had never been seriously ill. She often worked, only stopping when her energy ran out or a headache interrupted her schedule, but not for long. The years had not been easy ones. Earl had been born with a birth defect that required multiple surgeries on his leg which also meant hours and weeks at the hospital. The recovery time at home had been exhausting. In a flash of time Rosanna's mind went back to the the early days of her married life. The thoughts were with her as she gently rocked her precious baby Mary, who was content, cradled in her arms.

Chapter 2

1886

I

James and Rosanna had not known each other very long when one drizzly autumn day he had presented her with the idea that they seemed very well suited for one another. He believed this was a key factor for a good, sound marriage. It was not the customary marriage proposal for a young lady to receive in the nineteenth century. James was not a young man kneeling on one knee with star dust in his eyes and scared to death his heart might be broken by a refusal. There were no flowers nor a glittering engagement ring. But Rosanna had known his heart and his intentions were very sincere.

They both had been born and raised on a farm and came from large families. They knew what was expected from the demands of farm life: early hours, hard work, endless chores that kept one busy from sun up to sundown. There was never a guarantee of producing a successful crop. A good year depended on whether or not a crop received enough rain and not too much rain. The temperature needed to be just right, not get too hot or too cold. And if the weather cooperated, the crops were subject to other enemies: disease, pests and hungry critters. The tending of the livestock was also a never ending job. They, too, were subject to disease, accidents and attacks from wild beasts. There was always the risk of an accident or illness to fall on the farmer, his wife, his children (if so blessed with a family) and any farm hands that might be employed.

Yet, it was this life that the majority of Americans lived in the nineteenth century. It was the heart beat of the country. This was the life James and Rosanna chose to begin together as husband and wife.

They moved from Indiana to Illinois. James had put a down payment on a small farm. It wasn't long before they were expecting their first child. Rosanna remembered it so clearly.

Her labor pains had begun on February 29 in the year 1888. She had gotten out of bed, grabbed her shawl and wrapped it around her shoulders in an effort to ward off the bone chilling cold that had a way of creeping through the slightest openings in their wood frame farm house; between the wood slat walls, under the front and back doors, through the window frames and even up through the floor boards.

Winters in Illinois were never known to be mild. In an average winter, forty degrees Fahrenheit would be the high for the day and the lows were at least twenty degrees below that. All Rosanna knew was that she was cold! The tip of her nose turned red and wouldn't stop running. She had to keep dabbing it with her handkerchief. Her fingertips tingled with the coldness in the room. She kept pulling the long sleeves of her nightgown down to cover them, hoping it would provide a little warmth. Her whole body was shivering as she made her way to the wood stove. James had carefully kept the embers well fueled so they would burn through the night. He had the wood stove stocked with good, dry wood to be easily lit in the morning. Rosanna struck a match and soon had a nice fire blazing in the stove. She was grateful for her husband's forethought and preparations. It made her chore an easy one. The warmth eventually stopped her body from shivering. Her nose turned back to its normal color and the tingling in her fingers stopped. The coffee pot on the stove was already prepared with water and coffee grounds, just waiting for the burner to be lit and the nearly frozen water to start to boil. Soon the coffee would be brewing, bubbling hot and ready to drink. Rosanna felt if she could at least get something warm inside her body then maybe the pains wouldn't feel so sharp. Everything she did had to be done in between her labor pains which were now coming at regular intervals. With the heat from the stove, the hot coffee, and physical activity she was finally warming up nicely.

James woke up and could tell that Rosanna was experiencing some discomfort. He was upset she had not awakened him earlier. He quickly went to his wife and helped her back to the bed.

"Has it started?," he asked her.

"With this being my first, I'm not for certain," she answered, her words coming slowly.

He was worried there was not enough time to get their neighbor to come help with the delivery of their baby.

"Why didn't you wake me up the minute your pains started? Now I don't know if I should leave you and get Mrs. Schultz or stay here in case the baby is on its way. You shouldn't be alone."

James continued questioning her and expressing every concern he had while he quickly got dressed. As he finished putting on his socks and boots, he stood up and his short one-sided conversation stopped.

"I'm fine for now, James. Just put a kettle and pot of water on the stove before getting our neighbor, please. You'll be back by the time the water reaches a boiling point. If this is the real things, and not a false alarm, these pains could last for hours." she said. "But don't dawdle!," she quickly added.

James did as she instructed and got ready to leave. As James opened the door, a rush of cold air hit the room. Rosanna was surprised that it felt good, since she had spent a good part of the morning fighting the cold. She was now feeling warm and slightly flushed. The door closed, and as if it was a signal, a sudden, sharp pain caused her to double over. It took her breath away. Now she was questioning her own wisdom in sending her husband to get help.

Now all was ready. Rosanna was grateful James had left an ample supply of fresh, hot water. There were several pots and the large tea kettle filled to the brim simmering on the stove. For days, Rosanna had kept clean towels and sheets neatly folded and laid on the chair near the bed.

Rosanna regained her breath and decided to get out of bed. She thought it might help if she tried to resume some of her normal activity. Maybe it would take her mind off the pain. It was not a good idea. The next pain rendered her motionless and she barely made it back to her bed. This is how she was when James and Mrs. Schultz arrived.

By mid-afternoon Rosanna had no doubt this was the real thing. Clenching her teeth, she tried to suppress the screams.

Mrs. Schultz was by her side, gently stroking her dark hair from her face. "Let it go, girl. For some reason it seems to help. At least that's the way it was with me when having mine. It won't be long now, dear. You're doing good. I'm thinking you might be having a boy," said her kindly neighbor. Her opinion was quite convincing. Mrs. Schultz had eight of her own brood, five sons and three daughters.

James tried to stay busy. When he wasn't tending the livestock or checking on the water supply, he was pacing and staring at the closed bedroom door. It stressed him when he heard Rosanna in pain, and it frightened him when there was no noise at all coming from the bedroom. He decided to pack his pipe, thinking a good puff would help calm him, but since Rosanna and the coming baby filled his thoughts, he totally forgot to smoke his pipe. It remained in his hand as he paced back and forth.

By sunset, the sweet sound of a newborn baby's cries filled the house. Mrs. Schultz opened the bedroom door and told James, "You are now the father of a little boy. Come see. Your wife is doing fine."

But before he entered the room, his neighbor put her hand on his arm and looked into his eyes.

"The baby, he's strong, but all is not as good as hoped for."

James remained silent and went in to be with his wife and baby son. He found Rosanna holding the baby in her arms. A silent tear rolled down her cheek. He looked down at his newborn son and saw the reason for the new mother's tears. The baby boy was perfect in every way except for his legs. They had not developed normally, especially the right leg and foot. The leg was badly twisted and appeared disjointed. The tiny foot was barely recognizable as a foot, except for the five little buds that were his toes. The left leg gave the father hope that this child would not be completely crippled, but knew he would definitely be disabled. It was impossible for James to conceal his pain and concern from his wife, but somewhere deep inside he did find a few words to comfort Rosanna.

"We've been given a very special son." He wanted to say more but came up short on words to express his thoughts and feelings. All he knew was that he loved Rosanna and now they had a son to care for and love. They named him Earl.

II

Their little boy's early years had been very difficult. There were numerous visits to numerous doctors. Different opinions and different attempts to improve Earl's condition had been tried and failed. One such attempt could only be described as a living nightmare. Surgery had been done on both legs. He had been put in a primitive body brace and kept motionless for months. The theory behind the treatment was to let the legs heal, and hopefully, the condition would improve. Instead of improving, Earl's right leg had become inflamed. Infection set in and Earl experienced unbearable pain and a high fever. This had lasted several days. At one point the doctors had told Rosanna and James that the leg may have to be amputated. The parents had sat rigid in the doctor's office, trying to focus on the grim prognosis. At that time Rosanna was holding the then one year old Junieta, who at that moment was content playing with the ribbon on her mother's dress. James then nodded his head. He could hardly believe what the doctor was saying.

He thought, *We came here to help our son get better and now the doctors are telling us Earl might lose his leg, possibly lose his life.* James had looked at the doctor and said with a calmness that did not match the beating of his heart, "Be that as it may, about his leg. Save it if you can, but by God you better not lose our boy!"

Earl's leg had been saved, but it never healed properly. It was a miracle that the young boy was able to walk again after the surgery, but the walk was even worse. A noticeable limp and pain would be his constant companion the rest of his life.

Earl had adjusted to his handicap remarkably well. Though it slowed him down considerably, he persevered and concentrated more on what he could do rather than dwell on what he could not do. It was the stares and cutting remarks some people made that was the hardest for him to bear. Whether the remarks were made directly to his face or behind his back, the cruel words wounded him deeply. He built an invisible wall around himself to guard against the pain. He never allowed anyone to get too close to him, except for his family. They were his world, his sanctuary.

Chapter 3

1900

James pulled the wagon to the front of the house and called to Earl, "Better get a move on it, Son, if you want to get to your papers early." Earl nodded to his father then turned back to say goodby to his mother. With a wave and a grin, he said, "I'll see you later, Mama." The voice of her eldest son brought Rosanna's mind back to the present.

"Take care." She had a special smile for this boy of hers. It sometimes made him feel like he was five years old, not twelve. He didn't understand the special place he held in her heart. She didn't love him more than the other children. But she was extra proud of him. He had never had one normal day in his young life, yet he never felt sorry for himself. Everything he attempted he took as a challenge and was determined to succeed.

Rosanna turned her full attention back to the other children. They were now ready to move on to other activities. She needed to get the girls busy on their reading and sums. Being taught at home was a year round activity, but did ease up some during the summer. The girls had missed so much of their education due to a chronic illness.

The wagon ride to town did not take long. James and Earl rather enjoyed their ride together. They traveled the main street that followed the coast line. Earl especially never tired of hearing the rhythmic sound of the waves, as they rushed to the shore and then retreated back to the gulf. The high pitch of the sound of the sea gulls added to the choir of the beach. The comings and goings of the other citizens of Galveston also added to a sense of contentment. The constant activity signaled progress, a moving forward, toward a promising future. The only thing that slowed the population's movements and activities was the awful heat. Energy in the afternoon became understandably sluggish. Perhaps that was why the morning movements seemed to go doubly fast, people making up time in advance, knowing the afternoons would not be nearly as productive.

"Will you need a ride home?" James asked, as his son got down from the wagon.

"No thanks, I usually hitch a ride going that direction." Earl waved goodby to his father.

Earl was usually the first boy to get his bundle of papers. Because of his limp, he was much slower than the other boys delivering the papers. By being early, he got a head start; it was his compensation for the lack of speed. He was not the most out going boy, but he was the hardest working one, the most dependable one. He took great pride in knowing he was contributing to his family's financial well being.

He was always so glad to finish his route which placed him closer to home. Once at home, he would help his mother with chores and was especially helpful entertaining his younger brothers while his mother helped his sisters with their school work. He was still on summer vacation. He had one more week before school started in September. Junieta and Elgiva did not attend school, but had been tutored at home by his mother and father for years. At a very young age both girls had been diagnosed with Consumption.

Chapter 4

1895

I

It was this dreaded disease that brought the Steele family to Galveston, Texas. In the nineteenth century, Consumption, which was later named Tuberculosis, was the third most common cause of death in America. For Centuries it was called "Captain of Death". It was first thought to be hereditary, passed from one generation to another. It became a fact of life. Parents trained their children how to behave if they should become orphans and have to live with another family. The mere sound of a cough struck terror in the hearts of family members, fearing it was "Captain Death" and not the common cold. This is what happened when Junieta, age five, became dangerously ill.

It had started with a slight cough. Rosanna had been busy getting the children ready for bed. James had been studying for his exams. The family no longer lived on the farm. James had realized he was not cut out to be a farmer. His desire was to teach. So, by day he had worked in town at the local general store. At night he had been a student. Rosanna at that time was a full-time, over-time mother. James was gone most of the day and a good part of the evenings. The time he was home had been spent studying, This meant Rosanna carried the extra responsibilities fully on her shoulders. This was what a typical day looked like in the Steele home.

It was at the end of such a day. The children were in their night clothes, faces washed, teeth brushed,and tucked in bed. With their little tummies full, their little bodies tired from their day's activities, they should sleep soundly through the night. That was Rosanna's hope. She was exhausted and desperately needed a good night's rest, as was the case with most mothers of young children.

As she kissed her three children good night, she noticed Junieta's face looked a little flushed in the lamp light. Rosanna felt the child's forehead and sighed with relief.

"No fever tonight. That is good, my little "Junibug". Junieta looked up at her mother with a puzzled look on her face, but then wrinkled her little nose at the mention of her mother's nickname for her. Secretly she liked the name when her mother said it,but she didn't want her older brother, Earl to hear it. When he called her "Junibug" it sounded like he had a frog stuck in his throat. She would then put up a big fuss and the two children would have to be separated. Eventually, peace and calm would return in the family. Junieta didn't need to worry tonight. Earl was already soundly asleep. Rosanna placed a gentle kiss on her daughter's forehead and said good night.

All was calm now. The children were snuggly settled in bed, sleeping as only children can sleep. James was taking a short break from his studies. As was his habit,he went to sit in his favorite chair and filled his pipe to have a relaxing smoke.

He picked up a favorite book to do a little reading, just for enjoyment. Rosanna sat nearby and started working on her mending pile. She considered any job that allowed her to sit down to be a form of relaxation. She raised her eyes from her sewing and looked at James. She breathed in the sweet aroma coming from his pipe.

"This is nice, isn't it? The children safely sleeping, the house so quiet, a nice kind of quietness. Here we sit. Food in the pantry, a roof over our heads, and three healthy children. I think it is my favorite time of day."

James couldn't help but answer with a chuckle,which he didn't do very often, "It's no wonder you like this time of day, it's the only time you ever relax, if you call sewing relaxing. You only sit down to eat or hold one of the girls. Three children keep you busy."

"It may be four soon."

James put down his book, looked at his wife and asked, "Are you saying we're————"

"I'm saying what I've said three times before in our marriage. I think we're going to have another baby," Rosanna answered, a slight smile on her face.

James wasn't smiling, "But Elgiva is barely three."

"I'm fully aware of our children's ages," Rosanna answered him with no intention of being sarcastic. She was merely stressing the fact there was going to be another child, another mouth to feed, another little person to take care of, but most of all, another blessing. James had nothing else to say, but thought to himself, *So be it. We've always managed before.*

The two adults resumed their former activities; James picked up his book to read and Rosanna started to mend another sock.

Both of them retreating to their own thoughts. The house was still quiet. The only sound was the soft tick-tock of their clock sitting on a near by shelf. It was one of the few possessions that accompanied them when they had moved from the farm to the city. The clock and a small picture of a cottage covered in flowers and ivy with a poem about home went with them wherever they moved. Both had been wedding gifts from Rosanna's mother.

Then a slight, unexpected sound disturbed the silence. Rosanna turned her head toward the hallway, listening in case she heard again what she first thought she had heard.

By the second cough, Rosanna was on her feet going to check the children. She knew it was Junieta coughing. She could distinguish each child by their laugh, their cries, their little sighs, even when they were in another room. Junieta coughed again, but still had not awakened. Rosanna went to her child, and for a second time that night, felt her forehead. This time there was no doubt. Her little girl was running a fever. Rosanna gently lifted her daughter's head and propped her up a little higher on the pillow, hoping the position would help ease her coughing.

As Rosanna went back through the sitting room on her way to the kitchen, James noticed the expression on her face. He had seen it before. It was fear. He got up from his chair and followed her to the kitchen. She was at the sink filling the kettle with water. She heard James enter and without looking at him she said, barely above a whisper, "I'm going to make some honey tea for Junieta. It may soothe her throat and ease her cough before it gets too bad."

"I know what you're thinking, Rosanna, but it doesn't mean———."

"Don't tell me what 'it doesn't mean'," she snapped, still barely able to speak in a normal voice. The lump in her throat barely let her breathe, much less talk. "I'm sorry. I'm not angry with you. You know what I went through when my mother and sister were stricken with it and died. My God, James, you know there isn't one family we know that hasn't been robbed of a loved one by this monster! Why would you think we could be the exception?"

He went over to her and put his hand on her shoulder. She was trembling. "Come, sit down. I'll finish making the tea and I think you could use a cup yourself. I'll check on Junieta. Try not to worry. The children have coughed before and it was only a cold. I'll get the doctor in the morning."

She sat down and stirred some honey in her cup of tea. She took a sip, grateful for the warm liquid that helped relieve some of her tension. She watched her husband leave the kitchen. Then she set down her cup and put her head in her hands, rubbing her temples. For her, it was impossible to not worry. Junieta's cough this time sounded so much like her mother's and sister's cough when they struggled with Consumption. The memory of her mother and sister coughing themselves to death was still fresh in her memory, though it had happened years ago. Her mother had had the kind of Consumption that took years to kill its victim. Her sister had the other form that was called the Galloping Consumption, which entered not only the lungs, but the blood stream, and its victims died quickly. In some way it seemed a blessing, less suffering. Her mother battled the disease for three years before she succumbed to its brutal effects.

Rosanna remembered that when she wasn't trying to get her mother to eat or at least drink something, she was busy changing her mother's clothes and the bed linens. The hacking coughing which never stopped was always accompanied by blood and phlegm. Her poor mother had lost so much weight that her skin draped her bones much like the sheet draped her thin body. She had been only forty-five years old but looked seventy-five.

Every day Rosanna had gone to bed, short on sleep, long on exhaustion. She had told herself each night, *I've made it through one more day helping my mother. I've made it through one more day without experiencing a cough.* She had lived those days constantly wondering if she would inherit the disease. *It had already been passed to one sibling. Who would it claim next?*

Her mind quickly switched from the memories of her mother and sister of the past to her daughter. Now she may be facing the monster again. She thought to herself, *It is called Tuberculosis now, but Consumption is the better name. It truly totally consumed its victims.*

Her thoughts were interrupted when she realized James was speaking to her. He had returned to the kitchen.

"I think the tea helped Junieta. I hated waking her, but I think she'll rest better. She fell back to sleep fairly quickly and hasn't coughed for a while. How are you?"

Rosanna nodded her head and got up from the table. Not looking at James, she walked past him, telling him, "I'm alright. I'm going to get a wet rag and put it on Junieta's head and sit with her for a little while. Try to bring down her fever, then I'll come to bed."

An hour later James felt Rosanna quietly slip into bed beside him. He knew they were both relieved that Junieta had not had any more coughing spells. Her fever must have come down, otherwise Rosanna would still be with her. He kept very still, not wanting to disturb Rosanna. He knew how tired she was, how much she needed to rest. The minutes ticked away. James wasn't sure how much time had actually passed. He wasn't sure if Rosanna was asleep or not. She hadn't moved a muscle, but he didn't hear the deep steady breathing usually associated with sleep. He knew he was very tired and decided whatever was wrong with Junieta, a common cold or worse, they'd face it tomorrow. It didn't occur to him to put his arms around his wife and draw her close to him. It never occurred to him that Rosanna might have wanted to just be held, to feel his strength. He turned over and sleep came quickly to him. Rosanna was not as fortunate. It would be hours before her mind and body would surrender to sleep. Her pillow was wet with tears, after hours of silent weeping.

II

The morning sun rays showered the house, breaking through the early hours of darkness and sweeping away some of the gloom of the previous night. Rosanna had been up during those early hours, keeping a close watch on Junieta. There had been two more coughing episodes which were treated with the first remedy, honey tea with a little lemon juice added.

Rosanna got up from her bedside vigil and went to open the window slightly, to let some fresh air in to the room. She felt the warmth of the sun on her face and closed her eyes a moment to soak in its comfort. Her night time fears didn't seem as alarming in the light of day. For some reason she couldn't explain, problems did not seem as overwhelming in day light as they were at night.

She clung to a small thread of hope that Junieta suffered from the common cold, nothing more. James was getting ready to go get the doctor and have him check their daughter's condition. Rosanna kept telling herself, *The doctor will listen to Junieta's chest, look at her throat, take her temperature and then give them a bottle of his best potion for the* common *cold. This time next week Junieta would be well, playing with her doll and trying to be her little sister's second mother.* Rosanna also kept repeating to herself those old sayings ; '*Don't cross your bridges until you come to them, Don't put the cart before the horse*', and perhaps her favorite, '*Don't count your chickens before they've hatched*'. And wasn't there something in the Good Book about '*Living one day at a time, without looking for trouble in the next day*'?

Whatever the saying, it did help a little to loosen the invisible vise that gripped her heart. The best remedy for Rosanna to handle problems that were out of her control was to keep busy, which to be honest, was the norm for her. Earl and Elgiva would be waking up soon. Fortunately, Junieta was able to get some rest after her night of coughing.

Rosanna went to finish getting dressed. It didn't take long. She had put on her day clothes earlier that morning and slipped on her house slippers. Now she only had to put on her regular shoes and brush her hair, put it up in a quick bun, making herself presentable for when the doctor arrived. She then went to the kitchen to start a fresh pot of coffee. Doctors always appreciated a good cup of coffee. It seemed to rank high on their food chain. Rosanna knew it was a priority on hers. James and the doctor should be arriving soon.

Earl came through the kitchen door, half awake. His hair was tousled, going in a hundred different directions.

"Earl, go comb your hair and get dressed. Your father will be here soon with the doctor. I don't want you to look like some little street urchin that wandered into our house."

Earl hung his head. "Oh, Mama." Without any further comment he turned around and went to do as he was told. In a short time he returned, a little improved. But Rosanna didn't expect a lot from a seven year old boy.

"Sit down, Son," Rosanna said in a gentler tone. "I've got some bread and jam for you. Here is some coffee. Go easy on the sugar and cream. I want to have enough for the doctor," Rosanna told him.

"Thank you, Mama."

Rosanna poured herself a cup of coffee, and the mother and son sat at the table together, neither one speaking. Earl still wasn't fully awake and his total focus was enjoying his bread and homemade jam. Rosanna's mind was still on Junieta and thinking the doctor should be here by now. She was having difficulty trying to patiently wait for him.

III

The doctor arrived and it didn't take long to exam Junieta. Rosanna thought it took hours. For her, everything seemed to be moving in slow motion. The next thing she knew, Dr. Morrison was sitting at their kitchen table, his hands curled around a hot mug of coffee. He then set down his cup and folded his hands, keeping his elbows resting on the table. He found it hard to look at the two worried parents sitting across the table from him. It was never easy when there was bad news to tell them.

He began, "I have to tell you, I don't like the sound of her cough and she's having a little difficulty breathing. I think I heard some sounds in her lungs that could mean trouble. Now, I don't want to alarm you."

Rosanna thought to herself, *Too late for that. I'm scared out of my mind!*

The doctor continued, "But I don't want to give you any false hope either. I'm going to swab her throat. We'll have to wait and see what results we get. Have any of the other children or you or James had a cough?"

"Elgiva had a little cough this morning but no other symptoms." Rosanna was busy jostling Elgiva on her knee, trying to keep her quiet. "You're not thinking she could be sick too, are you?" Rosanna said with a voice filled with anxiety, nearing a state of panic.

"No, I'm just making sure no one else needs medicine while I'm here. I will take a swab of her throat and will run some tests on her also. It saves both of us time and me an extra trip. I will come back in a couple of days to check on Junieta. Hopefully, she's my only patient. I'm going to leave some cough syrup and something to help her rest. In the meantime, Rosanna, I want you to get some rest or you'll be one of my patients."

Dr. Morrison gave the mentioned medicine to the parents and prepared to leave. As he was putting on his coat, he said,

"There's really no sense to worry until we know for a certainty what is causing that cough. It'll take about a week before I'll be able to get back with you with the test results. I would admit her to the hospital if I thought that was the best place for her, but there is so much sickness going around, I think she's much better staying home. I know she'll get the best of care here. We've got more cases than I've seen in a long time and too few hands to help. I'm sorry." With those words Dr. Morrison left the house, got in his buggy and turned his horse around to head back to his office.

"Well, that's that for now." James told his wife. James turns to Earl and says, "Son, let's go check the chickens." He picked up the basket and handed it to Earl.

Rosanna was now left alone in the kitchen. The two girls were in their beds. Junieta fell fast asleep after the doctor left. Elgiva was back in her crib. She was wide awake and content after having her breakfast. In her crib, she busily played with her sock doll.

The young mother cleared the table, then poured herself another cup of coffee. She took a sip, having to force the liquid down her throat which seemed to have closed on her. Her eyes were filling with tears, which she tried to force back. She feared if she let one tear escape, it would open a dam of uncontrollable weeping. She took another sip and lifted her eyes to the ceiling, seeking an unseen God somewhere beyond the rafters.

"God, if you're there you've got to hear me. I feel I'm about to go insane. And I don't even know if the girls have a simple cold or——."

She couldn't say the word but her mind was shouting, *CONSUMPTION!* She continued her plea to God, "Just help us please. I don't know what I'll do if they are really sick."

Rosanna's short conversation with the Lord seemed to calm her for the moment. Although she didn't know very much about

God, she knew He was more powerful, stronger than she was and right now she needed that strength.

IV

Five days later, in the evening right after dinner, the doctor parked his buggy in front of the Steele home. He walked up the steps and knocked on the door. James welcomed the doctor into the parlor and offered him a chair.

"I'll go get Rosanna. Can I get you something to drink?"

"A cup of Rosanna's good coffee would be appreciated. There's a chill in the air and I've got a long night ahead of me."

James nodded and said, "I'll be back in a minute. Rosanna is checking on Junieta. We'll be right with you."

The three adults were seated in the parlor. The doctor was the only one with a cup in his hand. James and Rosanna sat together on the settee. James had one arm around Rosanna's shoulder and held her clenched hands with his other hand. They both seemed to be holding on to each other, to keep each other steady. They could already sense the doctor did not have good news. They had seen similar expressions on various faces of other doctors over the years. They were not strangers to hard news, a fact which didn't make it any easier. Before the doctor had a chance to speak, little Elgiva waddled into the room, holding her doll. She climbed up into Rosanna's lap with a little help from her father. Even at her young age, the little girl could sense something was not right. She sat there with her little arms wrapped around her mother's neck, rearranging her father's arms in the process. The child was unusually quiet, her lower lip starting to quiver. Rosanna hugged her little girl close to her heart. "It's ok baby girl. The doctor is going to tell us how we can get you and Junieta well." Elgiva looked up at her mother, not understanding what her mother was talking about, but knew her mother's voice sounded different. The young child buried her head in her mother's neck.

Rosanna put her hand on Elgiva's head to reassure her everything was fine. She loved the feel of her daughter's soft golden curls.

Dr. Morrison cleared his throat and said, "The test results came back today. It's what we feared. It is Tuberculosis."

"Both girls?" James interrupted the doctor.

"I'm afraid so." He answered.

Rosanna choked back a sob, but kept a steady stare on the doctor, waiting to hear what else he had to say.

"Now, what I don't know yet, is which kind they may have. You may be familiar with the two types."

Both James and Rosanna nodded their head. They knew all too well about this monstrous disease.

Dr. Morrison continued, "I want you to think about some different treatment options to consider. There's been some encouraging reports about people afflicted with Tuberculosis being cured or at least prolonged life without the severe side effects of the disease. My first recommendation is to move out of the city. Since the discovery that the disease is not hereditary, but spread by germs, we've also discovered it seems that large, heavily populated areas have a higher rate of cases. If there's any way to go west to the mountains or to a place near the sea, it may be very beneficial. If you can't see your way clear to make a move, then I'll make arrangements to have your daughters go for daily treatments. There are several areas in the city where the girls can get treatment."

Dr. Morrison was referring to "camps" which were set up in different sections of the city. These camps were basically rows of beds set outside in order to expose patients to as much fresh air as possible as long as the weather cooperated. Every patient was given a steady diet of fresh milk and eggs, thinking it would help boost their immune system.

For the first time since hearing the grim news of her daughters' condition, Rosanna's eyes seemed to have a spark of hope in them. She was unfamiliar with these most recent suggestions on the treatment of Consumption. She had a difficult time using the new name, Tuberculosis, for the horrible disease. Whatever its name, she hated it! At least now the doctor had given them a lifeline to hold onto, to keep the family from drowning in a deep, dark sea of despair.

James shook Dr. Morrison's hand and walked him to the door. "Thank you for your help. You've given us a lot to think about, decisions to make."

Dr. Morrison said, "I'll check back with you in a few days to see what you'd like to do. I don't have to tell you expediency is of great importance."

James nodded his agreement and closed the door.

The doctor was right. James and Rosanna knew that they needed to consider their options and make a decision as soon as possible. The one thing they knew without any hesitancy, was they did not want their children to be sent to one of the day camps mentioned. They didn't want the girls out of their sight. They were so young. That narrowed their choices of what to do down to one, where to move the family. Where would it be possible to make a new home and get their little girls well?

V

The next morning Rosanna woke up before the sun rose from its nightly nap. The cock's crow signaled that dawn was on its way. She sat up in bed and ran her fingers through her long, dark hair. She had been so tired the night before she didn't take the time to braid it. Now it would take her twice as long to get her hair under control this morning, but that was the least of her problems. She and James had a lot to think about, a lot of decisions to be made.

For the time being the ordinary demands of daily life would take up its usual amount of time, leaving little room to do extensive research on where and when to make their move. Getting dressed was first on her list. Next would be to check on the children, make sure the girls were still resting. They had had a better night last night. Their coughing was better since taking the medicine Dr. Morrison had prescribed. She would get breakfast ready before waking Earl. His schedule had been sadly disrupted by nights of little sleep due to his sisters' coughing, especially Junieta's. There had been nights her coughing seemed to be endless. Rosanna was so grateful for the restful relief the medicine brought to her little girl and the whole family.

James planned to take Earl to work with him. Today he was going to be busy restocking the shelves and Mr. Reed didn't mind the little boy's company. He was a help and didn't get in the way. It also allowed a little relief for Rosanna. She felt guilty that she couldn't spend more time with her oldest child. It took all her energy to take care of the girls. Today Rosanna wanted Earl to have a little extra rest. She would feed the hens and check for eggs this morning. That had been one of Earl's responsibilities over the last few weeks.

An hour later when Earl, now awake, started to rush out the back door to feed the hens and gather the eggs, Rosanna caught his arm to stop him.

"Mama, I've got to hurry! You let me sleep too long. I'm gonna be late. Then Papa won't take me with him," he anxiously told his mother.

"No, you're not going to be late. The hens have been attended," She told her son, smiling as she saw the relief wash over his face.

"Thanks, Mama. But_____"

"No 'buts' about it, Son. You are very welcome. You needed the rest and I can't have you getting sick on me. You are a big help to your father and me. I want to keep it that way. Now sit down while I get your breakfast. You can help get the lunches ready.

By the time Earl finished his breakfast, his sisters were awake. He was still at the table when Rosanna came in the kitchen, holding Elgiva on her hip. As she put the chunky little toddler in the highchair, she told Earl to watch his sister for a minute while she took some food to Junieta. In the meantime, he wrapped some bread in a napkin and got some fruit. He quickly stuffed both lunches in his coat pockets and was about to go tell his mother goodbye, but then remembered he was supposed to keep an eye on his little sister. Elgiva,who in the same amount of time had been busy, also. She had jam everywhere- on her face, in her hair, all over the high chair tray and arms. She was trying, unsuccessfully, to get the very last morsel off the tray with her chubby little fingers. Earl wet a rag and proceeded to clean his sister's face and hands, knowing she would make a big fuss. Half way through his attempt and Elgiva's protests, he decided to leave her alone. Immediate happiness returned. Earl made a mental note to himself, *A happy baby is a quiet baby,* even if the 'baby' was almost three years old.

James had pulled the wagon up to the house and there wasn't a minute to spare if he and Earl were going to be on time for work. He started to call out for his son, but got down from the wagon and walked up the front steps.

Being late this one time wouldn't hurt. He couldn't rush away to leave Rosanna alone to face the previous night's news.

He found her sitting on Junieta's bed trying to give some medicine to their little girl. She had eaten a little breakfast and the medicine would set better with some food in her stomach.

Rosanna was surprised to see him standing there in the doorway. She knew his insistence on punctuality. He should have been on his way to the store ages ago,

"You're going to be late. Earl is ready."

"I know. I just wanted to check on you. We've hardly had time to say ten words to each other since last night," he said. "It's a hard way to start the day and I just wanted to tell you we're going to get through this."

She nodded her head, trying to agree with her well meaning husband. His words reached her brain, but not her heart—at least not yet.

He patted her on the shoulder, "We'll talk when I get home."

Rosanna heard the door close as James and Earl finally left for town. She went to the window and watched the wagon as it rolled away down the dirt road.

She was left alone with Junieta and Elgiva. *Elgiva!* She loudly reminded herself as she rushed to the kitchen. Elgiva was still in her high chair. "Oh, my poor baby! Did you wonder where everybody went? I'm surprised you didn't try to get down by yourself." There was little chance of that happening. Since Earl had decided to leave her happily finishing her bread and jam, she was still content cleaning her tray of the very last speck of food.

"My goodness, Elgiva, you need a bath! No time for one now." Rosanna had to laugh at the sight of Elgiva's face, which was hardly recognizable behind the mask of jam. A swift rub with a wet rag was sufficient to clean the little face, hands, arms, and any sticky skin. It was going to take a bath to get the jam out of Elgiva's curls, but it would have to be later.

There would be no trouble keeping busy until the evening when she and James could sit down and discuss their situation. Years ago Earl's special needs had taken them on a 'journey' neither of them had ever imagined. Now their life was about to change again to meet the needs of their little girls. They would embark on another unimaginable experience.

VI

For the next few days one could set their clocks by either the setting sun or by the actions of James Steele.

Every evening after the dinner dishes were cleared, he would get a cup of coffee, gather his stack of newspapers and start searching for any information about possible places in the country where there might be a possibility of finding help for Junieta and Elgiva. Once he and Rosanna decided where to go, the other decisions would fall in to place. That was their hope. There would be a lot to consider.

They were currently renting their home. He felt there would not be a problem breaking their lease once the situation was explained to their landlady, Mrs. Cox. She was fond of the Steele family and had a soft spot in her heart for the children. Mildred Cox was a widow, having lost her husband to Consumption in the early years of their marriage. She had one son who was now living in another state. The Steele family filled a gap in her heart and James knew she would hate to see them go. The great challenge now was to decide on where to go; then find a job and a sufficient house, big enough to accommodate a family of five.

James focused on the newspaper spread in front of him. He searched the ads and articles that seemed to dominate a good portion of the paper. It beckoned people battling Consumption.

'COME WEST TO THE CLEAN MOUNTAIN AIR.
BE CURED'

or

"Rosanna, listen to this one." He read:

LET US CURE TUBERCULOSIS. SUNSHINE,
SALT AIR. IT'S THE ANSWER. BEST
SANATORIUMS IN THE COUNTRY. COME NOW
TO GALVESTON, TEXAS!

"Doesn't Mrs. Cox have a son who lives in Texas?" He asked.

Rosanna looked up from her mending, now done in the kitchen, ready to keep James company and be available for any discussion that might arise.

"I believe so, but I'm not sure where in Texas. I'll ask her tomorrow. She's coming for a visit."

"That will be good." James took a last sip of coffee and folded the newspapers. "I think I'm going to call it a day. Are you ready to go to bed?"

"I'll be there in a few minutes," Rosanna answered.

She put away her mending and got a small Bible from the bottom of her sewing basket. She had started reading a few pages every day for the last week. James didn't know about her night time reading, especially since it was the Bible. He didn't have a high opinion of religion. He considered 'religious' people as being weak and the ones who used the Bible as a crutch were the weakest.

Well, Rosanna had told herself, *I am definitely pretty weak right now. I've got to find some strength somewhere.*

She had voiced these thoughts to Mrs. Cox during one of their earlier visits. Mrs. Cox had then taken hold of the troubled young mother's hands and said, "Let me ask you, dear, do you believe in God, the Divine Being who created you and loves you?"

Rosanna hadn't known how to answer her friend. No one had ever asked her that question. She felt very uncomfortable and squirmed a little in her chair.

She finally replied, "I know about God. My parents took us to church sometimes. I guess I believe there's a God. But He's up there and I'm down here. I just never thought I could bother him with my problems."

Mrs. Cox had looked at her young friend. Rosanna felt like the older woman was using her warm, brown eyes to search her very soul. Then she heard her kind friend say something like, "Let me tell you this. I know there is a God and He's very much interested in you. Rosanna, let me ask you this. When one of your children has a problem, don't you want them to come to you and ask for your help? Of course you do." Rosanna nodded a yes. Her friend continued, "There isn't a problem too big for God to handle. He wants you to come to him for everything. But right now it isn't important what I believe. It's what you believe that's important. The next time I see you I'm going to bring you something."

Mrs. Cox was true to her word. That's how Rosanna happened to have the Bible she was now reading. She tried snatching moments of time during the day to read, but was more successful when everyone had gone to bed; it was the only time the house was quiet. James had never complained about the short time she took for herself at the end of the day. She did feel some guilt about her 'secret', but for the moment she didn't want any tension between them. He had enough to think about for the present. She wasn't afraid of her husband, but was afraid of what he might say to her. She wasn't sure if she believed what she was reading, but she knew the words made her feel better. She now closed the book and went to bed.

VII

The next morning Rosanna woke up with a feeling of great joy. She had had a good night's rest. It seemed the medicine was helping the girls and they actually slept through the night. It had been weeks since they had had an uninterrupted night of rest. But it was something more that gave Rosanna this wonderful feeling. It was hope. She knew James was close to making a decision about where to move, a place that would help their little girls get well.

Rosanna felt lighter on her feet. The heavy weight she'd been carrying in her chest seemed to be lighter also. She busily made breakfast, even humming the tune to an old hymn she remembered from her childhood, perhaps the only one she had ever learned.

> "What a friend we have in Jesus,
> All our sins and grief to bear!
> What a privilege to carry,
> Everything to God in prayer!
> Oh, what peace we often forfeit,
> Oh, what needless pain we bear,
> All because we do not carry
> Everything to God in prayer."

"What's that you're singing?" James asked.

Rosanna had been so preoccupied in her lightheartedness, she hadn't heard James enter the kitchen.

"Oh, just a little song I learned many years ago as a young girl," she answered. She set a bowl of porridge and a cup of coffee on the table just as James pulled out a chair and sat down.

She turned and went back to the stove to pour a cup of coffee for herself. As she joined James at the table, she said, "Let's take the children on an outing. We could have a picnic. It's such a beautiful day."

James started to object, "I don't think_____".

Rosanna quickly stopped him in mid-sentence, "Oh, I know you're thinking the girls aren't well enough, but don't you think the sunshine and fresh air will be good for them? That's what we keep reading about in all the ads night after night."

It was the beginning of Spring. Trees were turning green. Flowers 'first blooms were opening, their splashes of color accenting walkways and the nearby fields. Birds were singing their sweet songs announcing Winter was gone, Spring had arrived. The sunshine draped its warmth over everything it touched.

James was softening, but still was concerned, "It's still a little cool and there's a breeze that might be too much for the girls."

"We can wrap the girls warmly in blankets," Rosanna responded and added, "Earl needs some fun, also. He's been cooped up almost as much as the girls."

"Well, maybe so, but I can't picture Elgiva staying wrapped up for long."

Rosanna had to agree, but also offered, "We don't have to stay out very long. It may be our last chance for a while. We'll soon be getting ready to move. There'll be no time for a picnic then. Please, James," she pleaded so convincingly. The happiness on her face went straight to James's heart. He couldn't refuse such a request. He got up from the table and pushed back his chair, "I'll get my chores done and be back to help get the children ready for your picnic." He started to leave the kitchen, but stopped and turned around to face Rosanna. He said, with a puzzled expression on his face, "Wait a minute. Who said we were getting ready to move soon? We haven't even talked about where we plan to move, much less when."

"I could tell last night from the way you put away the newspaper. You had a certain look, almost peaceful, on your face," Rosanna said.

"We'll talk about it later," James started to leave.

Rosanna rushed toward him and caught him by the elbow.

"Oh no you don't. You're surely not going to leave me hanging. Tell me now what you're thinking. Where are we moving? We can 'discuss' the details later."

James couldn't refuse her. "I'm thinking about Texas, the city of Galveston. It's an island in the Gulf of Mexico." With that said, he left to go do some work.

Texas, hmm, that puts a bee in my bonnet; gives me a lot to think about, Rosanna said to herself as she went to wake up the children. She was excited to tell them about the day's plans. She would have to try to set aside her thoughts about Texas. She needed to focus on getting ready for the picnic.

VIII

James and Rosanna sat at the kitchen table, that evening. The picnic had turned out to be a wonderful idea. The girls had enjoyed being outside. When Rosanna had tucked them in bed that night she thought she saw that a little color had come back to their cheeks. Earl, also had a good time exploring the surrounding area. Rosanna couldn't help but think how well Earl managed with his physical limitations. Although he couldn't run or climb the trees and rocks, he still found other ways to investigate the assortment of creatures nature provided for a young boy equipped with a keen curiosity and a vivid imagination.

Now she turned her full attention to James. He had spread out a map on the table. He was ready to share his plan with Rosanna. He was sure, or practically sure, she would agree. He confidently began to tell her about Galveston, Texas and all the promise it held for his family. He also hoped that the fact Mrs. Cox's son, Robert who lived in Texas, would be a big help. He had contacts in Galveston that possibly could help James secure a job and find adequate living quarters for his growing family. The city itself had a lot to offer. It was becoming the 'New York City' of the South.

In 1894 Galveston, Texas was a city of lights. The streets were lighted by electricity, the first city in Texas to have such a claim. There was the telegraph, the telephone, and a streetcar system. Many of the public buildings had a turban-drive power system. Some places had the luxury of flush toilets. One of the main attractions for James was Galveston was known to be one of the cleanest cities in the country; very important for those who were infected with Tuberculosis. There were more millionaires per capita in Galveston than any other city in the United States.

Although the Steele family was not in that category, it was another important factor to them. A wealthy community meant a thriving community which translated in to more job availabilities. Employers meant workers were needed; salaries would be paid for the working population, which was growing at a tremendous rate. The increase in a population also meant families with children needed schools and schools needed teachers. This made James very optimistic. There was one draw back from all this burst of growth. The housing industry was having a hard time providing accommodations for the thousands of newcomers moving to Galveston annually.

A few hundred years earlier you could not pay any civilized human being to live on the island. It was practically impossible to imagine a large population inhabiting such a small area. It was a mere 'sliver of land' with the highest point being only eight feet above sea level. The very definition of an island is an area of land surrounded by water. To the north of Galveston was the bay, to the South was the Gulf of Mexico. The island had once had the name, Snake Island, named by the Karankawa Indians. The snakes and the Indians were the main inhabitants on the island.

By the nineteenth century the white settlers began to move to Texas, coming by land and by sea. The Steele family was a part of this group. There were many people like them, moving to the Texas sea coast, seeking a cure for Tuberculosis.

IX

The journey to Texas had not been an easy one. James and Rosanna sold most of their belongings to help fund the cost of moving. It also helped simplify their move. They kept a few family heirlooms, packing them carefully in their trunk, protected between the bed linens, blankets and clothes. Earl carried one bag which had his clothes and a treasure or two of his own. With careful planning, Rosanna was able to pack the rest of the family's clothing in three bags. This was no easy feat for a family of five.

They had mapped their route allowing for frequent stops along the hundreds of miles journey. They set specific goals of intended distances divided by the number of days they thought was needed to arrive at their destination. They also knew their schedule would be subject to change, depending on the physical condition of Junieta and Elgiva. One could never predict when the girls might have a bad day and in most cases their bad days were rarely on the same day. There was also a factor James and Rosanna now had to consider in their plans. They were happily expecting their fourth child, but this time Rosanna suffered from debilitating headaches. The severity of these headaches was a new experience for her. When they first hit, she thought it was the stress of the move, but deep down she knew it was not stress causing the headaches. This move was filled with high expectations and an abundance of hope for a better future for their daughters. She would gladly welcome a new child in the family, but was apprehensive of the timing. The girls' diagnosis and the need to move had all happened in a very short amount of time. She also knew deep down that somehow things always worked out one way or the other.

Whether from the journey or the baby, she traveled the great distance often holding a wet rag to her forehead with one hand and trying to tend to Elgiva with the other hand. Husband and Wife sat across from one another on the train. Earl sat by his mother, next to the window. He was content staring at the quickly changing scene. Junieta happily played with her doll and didn't care where she sat. The train chugged along, rocking its occupants from side to side.

"I wish I could help you feel better," James said, looking at his wife helplessly. He stretched out his hands and told Rosanna, "Here, let me take Elgiva." He lifted the little girl and placed her on his knee, bouncing her. She giggled with delight as her father recited the well worn words, "This is the way the farmer rides, 'Clippity clop, clippity clop.' Changing the rhythm of the bounce he continued, 'This is the way the gentleman rides, Flippity flop, flippity flop.'" And lastly, with a gentle bounce, "'The is the way the lady rides, Trippty trip, Trippity trip, as they all went to town, to town.' "He then scooted closer to the window to let Elgiva watch the scenery whiz past them. She clapped her hands and giggled with excitement. Now Junieta wanted a ride on her papa's knee. James was obliged to grant her request.

For the first time that day Rosanna managed a smile. She looked at James and said, "You keep this up and you're going to be the one with a headache." James barely heard her above the clacking of the train wheels which drowned out her words.

He actually read her lips more than he heard her.

It was good to see her smile. Finished with Junieta's ride, he thought to himself, *More like my knees are going to give out rather than suffer a headache.* At least they were on the 'last leg' of their trip. They were scheduled to arrive that afternoon.

The plan was to go directly to the rental house Robert Cox had found for them. Rosanna had no anxiety about the new residence. She was too preoccupied with the children and her headache to have any thoughts about their new home. She was hoping to feel better once she got off the train. The noise did not help her condition.

James was apprehensive enough for both of them. This was the first time he had ever moved his family to a place he had not seen. He was putting a lot of faith and trust in Mrs. Cox's son, Robert. The young man had been so kind and helpful, it was easy to like him and thus trust him. James calmed his worries by reminding himself that this move probably was not going to be a permanent one; the house was rental property. If Rosanna did not like it, they could look for a house she liked better. One of the qualities James admired about his wife was she wasn't particularly particular. She had a talent for making the best of most situations. He felt confident she would do the same now.

Their travels finally came to an end. As the Steele family departed the train, the two adults felt as if they were stepping in to a foreign country. Even though they had been told it was normal to see diversity on a grand scale in a port city, they were still shocked. If James and Rosanna had ever gone to New York City they would have seen the same interesting diversity, but on an even greater scale. The ad they had read about Galveston was accurate, it truly was the 'New York City' of the South!

This was home now. Rosanna found the house adequate, but she did wish it was one room larger. But it would do. It was located in the northwest part of the city, near the bay. Their route took them along the Gulf side of the city, giving them their first view of the ocean. The great mass of water awed them all.

'Papa, that's the biggest pond I've ever seen!" Junieta being the first to say anything about their new home town.

Rosanna smiled at Junieta's words and gave her a hug. There was something frightening about being on an island, surrounded by so much water. She was relieved when James told her their house was near the Bay. It too, held a lot of water but you knew land was a short distance on the other side. She didn't mind one bit not being near the beach. It mattered to some people, but not Rosanna. Her first impression of the ocean was it was an overwhelming amount of water. It thrilled her to look at it, but it also frightened her at the same time. There was so much unseen, unknown beneath its surface; a multitude of creatures she had never heard of much less seen that lived there. She pictured it being forever dark; never seeing the sun or the stars sparkling in the sky. She supposed some people felt fearful about forests and mountains which had their own mysterious creatures and terrain. Yet, in her mind it was easier to understand things of the land because you could see your surroundings, your feet were on solid ground. Your eyes could see the sky above, the moon, the stars that spread its canopy over the earth at night. You could feel the sun and its rays that painted the earth, giving life its warmth. Though this part of creation held its own element of the unknown, it was a part of your world; plants, all the creatures breathed air with their lungs. She was one of the land creatures, The ocean was, to Rosanna, a different world.

Yes, she decided very quickly she preferred mountains over the ocean. It had been her hope that they could have moved farther west and let the girls breathe the fresh crisp mountain air she had heard about so much. The expense of such a move was the deciding factor. It had also puzzled her that they had decided on a location heavily populated; they had just moved from a large city. The doctor had told them that such an environment contributed to the spread of Tuberculosis. Then it was explained to her that the salt air, being near the ocean off set the growing population. Their decision was also helped tremendously by having a contact in Texas. She had also decided and resolved in her heart that she would spend the rest of her life here, in Galveston if her girls got well, if their Tuberculosis would go away.

Chapter 5

1900

I

Rosanna's thoughts had covered a lot of years in the short amount of time she had spent on the front porch, rocking Mary and watching the children play.

It was hard to believe they had been here five years, and had added three more children to the family. The Steele family was at the same address, but were in the process of trying to find a larger home. Their little home was adequate though, it seemed to be 'wall to wall' children. The family managed only because the three youngest children were small, ranging in age; four and a half years old, two years old and the three month old baby. As children normally grow, what seems to be rapidly, the family would soon find they had grown out of their house. James and Rosanna were trying to move before that happened. Rosanna had enjoyed the house hunting before Mary was born. It was fun, although very time consuming to look at different properties. She found a house that she believed would meet the family's needs. It was a two-story home and more centrally located in the city.

At night she would lay awake, imagining the family in their new surroundings. She'd pick a room for the girls, one which would be closest to her bedroom. She'd think carefully which one for the boys, and which room would be best for James and herself. She would glance around the parlor and place a chair and table by the window. She had seen the ideal fabric to make curtains for the windows. The settee would go beautifully along the wall between the other two windows in the room and above the settee she would hang a picture. She wished the house had a fireplace with a mantle; it would be the perfect place to put her pendulum clock. The tick-tock, tick-tock and gentle chimes of the clock which had filled the house every hour was one of her favorite sounds. But there wasn't a need for a fireplace in Galveston, especially in the smaller homes. The winters were mild and the stove in the kitchen was adequate to warm most of the house. Much of the furniture and accessories were also imaginary, a dream for the future. It was taking time and savings to slowly replace the furniture they had left behind when moving to Texas. Yet, Rosanna felt a peace and contentment in her heart she hadn't felt for a long time. Life was looking good for the growing family. Junieta and Elgiva were doing well living close to the sea. It had been a good decision. Even though the girls still had episodes of the illness that frightened them, the episodes were happening less frequently. This was a gift from Heaven. Earl had adapted well in his new surroundings. The three children she'd given birth to in the past five years were healthy and thriving. The family had settled into a comfortable, happy routine.

Rosanna decided it was time to get busy with the duties of the day. She got up from her chair and told Junieta and Elgiva it was time to get started with their school work.

"I'll put Mary in her crib and then we'll start on your numbers. Roy and Albert will make a good audience when we get to your reading. I'm surprised they sit still long enough for you to finish a story, but it shows what good readers you are. You hold their attention amazingly well."

"I think it's the stories you pick for us to read that they like, Mama," Junieta said.

Rosanna gathered the books, paper and pencils as the girls seated themselves in their usual places at the table.

"Well, maybe it's the combination." Rosanna said. "You know what surprises me? They like the true stories better than the make believe ones."

"I do, too,' Elgiva added.

"Whatever the reason, I'm grateful." Rosanna had the girls open their books and assigned them their arithmetic problems for the day. It was mainly review work from previous lessons. There would be plenty of time to tackle new concepts later in the week.

Galveston schools didn't start for another week. Earl was the only student from the Steele household to attend the public school. The girls had been taught by their parents since they were old enough to go to school. It was an advantage that James was a teacher and Rosanna, though not as formally educated as her husband, was highly intelligent and also had a good amount of patience. James and Rosanna were very guarded with their daughters and tried to keep them away from crowds. A school classroom, filled with children was a breeding ground for germs. It was not a good environment for anyone battling Tuberculosis.

II

Earl was fully aware how many days he had left before school started. One more week of no school, one more week of no worries about tests and homework. He was going to try and enjoy every minute of it. It was a well known fact Earl did not enjoy school. He enjoyed learning, but not within a four walled structure. He did not like sitting still at a desk for hours and the hardest part of all, having to listen to a teacher and try to remember what had been said. He learned best by "doing". Earl liked to explore the great outdoors. Since living in Galveston, he especially liked going to the beach and finding treasures in the sand or standing at the edge of the retreating waves. He was careful to never get too close to the water of the Gulf. He did not know how to swim and did not know if it was even possible for him to actually learn because of his leg. He wore his leg brace and special shoe as long as he was awake. He only took it off when he went to bed and when his mother forced him to take a bath.

If he wasn't at home, or at school, or delivering his papers, he was at the beach. He could spend hours watching something as simple as a crab, as it crawled this way, then that, using its six pairs of appendages to capture its food. He was especially interested in watching crabs fight one another. They were very aggressive little creatures. He sometimes made a secret bet on which one would win. He also enjoyed gathering sea shells for his sisters. There was an abundant supply and the girls were always excited to get one. With the larger ones they would hold the sea shell to their ear and listen to the soft, swooshing sound of the ocean. It was a marvelous, wonderful mystery to them. But for Earl, more than anything, he was in awe watching the waves; the heights they attained depending on the speed of the wind. There were times the great rushing waves would rise from the great body of water and appear as large, clutching claws reaching for the beach, sweeping it clean of anything they could, and then take their bounty back to the sea. Earl was always careful to not be within reach of its clutches. Other times the water would gently brush up onto the shore and lazily return to the sea with the same regularity as if inhaling and exhaling. At these times Earl would approach the very edge of the water and let it rush over his hands, just to feel its temperature.

It was on this day, during one of his explorations, that Earl noticed another boy on the beach, walking towards him. As the boy got closer, Earl recognized him. He was a boy that had attended school last year, but then hadn't been there when the term ended for the summer. Earl had wondered what had happened to him. He thought he had probably moved. They had not been friends, but had known each other by name. Earl didn't really have any close friends, either in or out of school. He kept to himself. By the young age of twelve the wall he had built around himself was taller and thicker. Years of being stared at, ridiculed and too often the brunt of cruel jokes and jesting, had forced him to build such a barrier. It was his way of self-preservation. The wall was not entirely of his own making or choice. His entire family kept very much to themselves.

In the mid-1890's it was discovered that Consumption was caused by the spreading of germs. It was not hereditary as had been believed for centuries. The name Consumption was replaced by the name Tuberculosis. With this new discovery that the disease was contagious, came the stigma on those who were afflicted. Earl had two sisters with Tuberculosis. Not many people knew of their illness. His parents deliberately sheltered the girls from others, for their sake and for the sake of others. His mother had become friends with their neighbor, Molly, who knew of the family's secret. She was a nurse and had been a big help to the family several times. His father had his fellow teachers, but no close friends. Earl didn't mind not having any friends. He had convinced himself he preferred it that way.

But now here was that boy walking directly towards him. *Oh, what's he coming here for?* Earl asked himself. It was too late to pretend he didn't see the boy. He had seen him and even nodded in recognition. *What's his name?* Earl's mind suddenly went blank as he tried to remember it. Now they were face to face. The 'boy' was the first to speak, "Hi. Aren't you Earl? I remember you from school."

Before answering, Earl thought cynically to himself, *Yeah I'm sure you remember me. Everybody remembers the guy with the bum leg.* Then Earl said, "I remember you too, but I forgot your name"

"It's Will, Will Murney."

"I haven't seen you in a while. Thought you had moved or something."

"No, I didn't move. Well, I did move but not far. My folks died so my younger brother and me had to go to the orphanage. Don't have any family to take care of us."

"That's too bad. Sorry to hear that." Earl didn't know what else to say.

Will went on and filled in a few details. "My mother was sick for a long time. She had Consumption, I mean Tuberculosis. She passed away and the next day my Pa had a heart attack. They were both gone, just like that!" Will snapped his fingers to describe the suddenness of his loss.

"What's it like, living at the orphanage?" Earl asked.

"Not too bad. The nuns are real nice and the food is pretty good. I'm glad I still have my little brother. I'd be awful lonesome without him."

On an impulse, Earl blurted out, "My two sisters have Consumption, I mean Tuberculosis. Right now they're doing pretty good. But my mother never leaves them out of her sight for long."

Will nodded his head, indicating he understood what it was like having a loved one suffering from the dreaded disease. "I didn't know you had sisters. Do they go to school? I don't ever remember seeing them."

Earl was starting to feel a bit uncomfortable, but quickly answered, "Oh, they're schooled at home. Just to be safe. Sometimes they almost seem well."

"That's great." Then Will decided to change the subject, much to Earl's relief. "What are you doing on the beach, hunting for coins? The out-of-towners drop them all the time."

"I do a lot of diggin', but only find sand dollars and sea shells, no coins, but I don't ever go to that area, too many people."

"Well, we could go there together sometime. I could help you look for coins." Will's offer seemed genuine.

Earl was still guarded in his conversation and could only say, "Yeah, maybe sometime. I gotta go now." He turned to go home.

Will wasn't that easy to dismiss. He ran after Earl and easily caught up with him. "Hey, where do you live? It looks like we're headed in the same direction." Will said. Both boys were walking west.

"Thatta way, near the bay." Earl looked at Will and pointed in the direction of his home.

"OK, I can walk part of the way with you. You know where the orphanage is, everybody does, I think."

"I know where it is." Then Earl did something he'd never done before. He asked Will if he'd like to meet at the beach the next Friday, after he got home and finished his chores. Will agreed. The boys were silent for the remainder of their walk, except to say, "See ya." Then Earl turned to go north, hoping he could catch a ride. It was a long way and his leg was starting to hurt. Will kept walking west, having to go a much shorter distance, since the orphanage was practically on the beach.

The rest of the way home, Earl questioned what he had just done. He thought to himself, *Will probably won't show up. He'll find something else to do. Or maybe he will meet me.* Earl barely dared to think, *Maybe I've made a friend.* His well built wall was cracking a little. It surprised him how good it felt just having the possibility of having a friend.

No one saw Earl's slight smile, but it came from that well of hope———-hope that Will might be a real friend. He hadn't stared at Earl's leg, or called him a hurtful name, or even felt uncomfortable talking with him. He treated Earl like he was just a regular guy. Will was genuinely nice. Earl was convinced he was walking better, faster than usual despite the pain, as he made his way home. Even going up the steps to his front porch seemed easier. Now his leg didn't seem to hurt at all.

When he entered the house he found everyone sitting at the table, ready to have dinner. He rushed to the sink to wash his hands, then took his usual place at the table. His father gave him a side glance as he finished passing the food to his family.

"You're late," his father said. "We waited on you as long as we could. You almost missed dinner and you've kept six good people waiting."

Earl stuttered slightly, trying to explain, "I, I lost track of time."

"Doing what?" His father asked gruffly. This shocked Earl. It was a side of his father he'd never seen, and a tone he had never heard.

"I ran into a boy from school, at the beach. We got to talkin' and time got away from me."

"You certainly did lose track of time. Unfortunately, the chickens and the cow don't 'lose track of time'. Get up and get out there now and tend to them. Your mother will have a plate ready for you when you get finished with your chores. But only this time. Next time you 'lose track of time', you'll lose your dinner. Do you understand?"

"Yes, Papa, I understand. It won't happen again, I promise." Earl got up from the table and left out the back door, but not without noticing the expression on his mother's face. There was sadness in her eyes. He knew she would have let him eat dinner with the family, then tend to his chores, but she never went against his father.

Rosanna considered her husband's way was better, harder sometimes, but better. Earl would likely never repeat this offense again. She only wished James' strictness this time could have been tempered with a little more mercy. Earl had seemed happy when he came home tonight. It had something to do with the meeting of his schoolmate on the beach. Earl never talked about being with any other boys at school. James was upset with Earl and it put a cloud over Earl's happiness.

It had been a while since Rosanna had been able to read her Bible. She did remind herself now, that God had mercy in abundance. She'd ask Him to give her husband some of it. Her lack of attention to her reading made her feel guilty, that she was letting God down in some way. But the bigger cause of feeling guilty was due to the fact she was still keeping it a secret from James.

Chapter 6

I

The first week of school passed with relatively little difficulty. Rosanna's routine was the same, except there was the new baby added to her responsibilities. Her days were fairly predictable. There was breakfast to prepare, household chores to be done, the girls' lessons to supervise, while at the same time try to keep Albert occupied and out of 'little boy trouble'. Roy had started going across the street twice a week to Mrs. Clarke's house to help with simple chores. It gave Rosanna a short break, and Mrs. Clarke enjoyed having Roy's company. The little two-year-old Albert didn't quite know what to do without his brother, Roy. Roy was his constant companion and always had something for them to do. Of course, it didn't always meet with their mother's approval. This new arrangement had only been in effect for one week and every day that Roy was gone, Albert would be waiting for him on the front steps of the porch. His dimpled elbows would be resting on his knees and his chin cupped in his chubby little hands, waiting for Roy to return. Then he'd practically fly off the steps and run to his brother when he did get home from Mrs. Clarke's. He would grab Roy's hand and literally pull him up the front steps, jabbering questions in the language of a two-year old. Roy was one of two people in the family that half understood what Albert was saying. Rosanna was the other one.

Then, of course there were all the needs of a new baby in the family. Somewhere in the never ending job of being a mother, Rosanna needed to find time to give James the attention a husband needed. Rosanna rarely thought about her own needs. Life was what it was and she didn't complain.

II

It was now Friday. The weekend would be just as busy, but in a different way. Rosanna was busy with her regular morning routine with the added preparations for tomorrow's day trip that James and Earl were taking. They planned to leave on the first train to the mainland and catch the last train returning to the island Saturday evening. The breakfast dishes were washed, dried and put away, with the help of Junieta and Elgiva. The girls then started on their school assignments. Roy and Albert were content playing with their blocks. Roy's imagination was a constant amazement to Rosanna. The simple wood blocks would become horses, often times exotic jungle animals or wagons, tall buildings, and sometimes people. The boys never seemed to tire of this world of blocks which often had sticks and rocks added to the scene. In many ways Albert seemed advanced for his age, but he also had the advantage of watching his older brother maneuver the countless objects they found to play with. Rosanna had finished the day's laundry, which was mainly Mary's diapers. They were hung on the line, drying quickly in the day's heat. They would soon be ready to fold.

Mary was taking her morning nap, but not peacefully. She seemed a little restless. The heat and a slight cough shortened her normal two hour nap. There was that phrase again, thought Rosanna, 'a slight cough'. Mary has 'a slight cough.' Many years ago her mother and sister had had 'a slight cough'. And not so many years ago Junieta and Elgiva had 'a slight cough'. All those coughs turned out to be Consumption. Rosanna knew the new name for the disease was Tuberculosis, and she said again to herself it would always be Consumption. She still described it as a disease that totally consumed its victims. Now she tried to concentrate on something else before her thoughts took her down the road to hysteria. Mary woke up from her nap. Rosanna changed her diaper and washed her with a cool rag. Mary seemed to enjoy being free of her clothing. Though she was only three months old she had a remarkable ability to express her comforts and discomforts.

Not knowing where the time went, it was now close to lunch time. Rosanna quickly got lunch ready for the children. After their meal, she put Roy and Albert down for their afternoon nap. Mary nursed happily and now, hopefully, she would take a better nap this afternoon.

Molly was coming over for a cup of coffee and her mother, Mrs. Clarke, had been invited, but had to decline; she had some volunteer work to do at the church. It was so nice to have such lovely, friendly, energetic friends that lived across the street. It was sometimes difficult to tell which had the most energy, mother or daughter. That convenience wasn't going to last much longer. Molly was engaged to be married and would soon be moving to a little house located near the hospital. There was a possibility Mrs. Clarke would move with her daughter. They would still be friends and have visits, it just wouldn't be as convenient. Rosanna would miss them greatly, but if the Steele family moved to the house Rosanna had found, the friends would be in walking distance of each other. Rosanna refused to think about that now. She was looking forward to Molly's visit today.

Rosanna filled the coffee pot and put it on the stove to heat and be ready by the time Molly was expected to arrive. She then got two of her best cups and saucers from the cupboard and set the table. A fresh batch of cookies had been baked early that morning. It would be a rare treat to have home baked cookies, for rarely did anyone bake anything during the heat of the season. Rosanna went to the front porch to make sure Molly wasn't on her way yet. There would be a few minutes for Rosanna to freshen her face and give a quick brush to her hair. After a quick glance in her mirror to check her appearance she went to check on Mary. Mary's afternoon nap didn't seem to be much better than the morning one. She drifted in and out of a fretful sleep. Rosanna softly walked over to the crib. "Poor little girl, you're so tired and need your rest. I know it's hard to settle down properly in this heat." Rosanna gently took off Mary's cotton baby dress, remembering how much Mary liked her freedom earlier that morning. Rosanna was overly cautious to not disturb her baby. She left only the diaper on, hoping if Mary was cooler it would help her rest better. The mother gently rubbed the small, soft back of her newest child. Was there any thing in the world softer to the touch than a baby's skin? Rosanna didn't think so. The gentle stroking helped Mary to relax and she finally drifted into a peaceful sleep, at least for a little while. Rosanna breathed a sigh of relief. The baby was asleep. Albert and Roy were napping. The girls were never any trouble, always content to read a favorite book or work on one of their crafts. Rosanna had started teaching them how to knit. With the house and the children in good order, she should be able to have a good visit with Molly.

Junieta stood at the bedroom door, about to tell her mother that Molly had arrived, but Rosanna quickly put her forefinger to her lips, signaling Junieta to be very quiet. Her oldest daughter recognized the gesture and whispered, "Miss Molly's here."

Rosanna smiled and followed her daughter out of the room.

Molly was in the parlor talking with Elgiva and admiring her handwriting exercise.

"Your handwriting looks like a work of art. I can read it so easily. A few of the doctors at the hospital could take lessons from you. I sometimes have trouble reading their notes on the patients' charts. They need to take lessons from you."

"Hello, Molly. I'm sorry I've kept you waiting. Mary's not having a very good day," said Rosanna.

"With this heat, I'm surprised anyone can get any rest, me thinks, young or old." Molly said in her charming British accent.

"So true, plus she has a slight cough." There was that phrase again, Rosanna thought as she and Molly made their way to the kitchen. Rosanna stopped to check on Junieta and Elgiva. "Girls, why don't you take a break. You've been at your lessons long enough. If you want to get out of the house, you may go out and play in the backyard. Make sure you stay in the shade," Rosanna cautioned the girls.

The girls gladly grabbed their dolls and rushed outside to play their version of 'Mommy'. They squealed in delight as they discovered to find their own tea party had been set up under the one tree in the backyard. Their mother had spread a small quilt under the tree. She had placed a small tea pot, two cups and saucers, and best of all, a plate of cookies on the quilt. They both giggled and ran back to give their mother a hug. Then they bounded down the steps to go enjoy their treats.

Rosanna and Molly stood on the back porch to watch the girls for a moment before getting their own visit started.

Molly said, "When in the world did you find time to do that?" Molly nodded in the direction of the girls in the back yard.

"I was up earlier than usual with Mary and thought it would be a nice change for them. I sometimes forget they are still little girls. So Mary and I got the party set up. Mary seemed to enjoy being outside. It seemed to relax her. I don't know if it was my wishful thinking, but it seemed a little cooler. I would have stayed out longer with her but had to get breakfast ready."

"There is a slight breeze coming from the North," said Molly.

"Well, now let's get that cup of coffee I promised you. What time do you have to be at the hospital?"

"Oh, not until tomorrow morning. I have the early bird shift. I traded with another nurse. I didn't mind. It means I'll have this evening free. David wants to take me to the beach house for dinner and a moonlight swim."

Rosanna smiled and said, "That sounds nice." She had never confessed to Molly her fear of the ocean.

The two women sat at the kitchen table, enjoying a relatively quiet house as they talked. Roy and Albert were still asleep, neither one had barely moved a muscle. Their constant motion in the mornings almost always guaranteed a good, long nap in the afternoons. Mary was still sleeping, coughing only a few times. Rosanna kept her head slightly turned towards the open door, always listening with one ear in case Mary's cough persisted and listening to Molly with her other ear.

Molly could tell that her friend was a bit distracted. "Has Mary had that cough very long?" Molly asked between sips of coffee. Her green eyes peering over the rim of her cup, trying to read Rosanna's expression. She knew how anxious her friend could get over the sound of a cough. She knew Rosanna was always on guard with Junieta and Elgiva. Rosanna had shared with Molly the girls had been diagnosed with Consumption at an early age. Molly also knew Rosanna had lost her mother and sister to the disease and that the family had moved to Galveston in hopes the sea air would help cure the little girls. Their health had improved, but they were not cured.

Rosanna finally answered her friend's question, "Not long at all. It started last night, but didn't really seem like a cough, more like she was trying to clear her tiny throat." She avoided looking at Molly, afraid her eyes would betray the fear that filled her heart. She didn't fool Molly, who then gently offered a word of encouragement while at the same time showing concern.

"Could be allergies or this awful heat. Why don't you and Mary come to the hospital with me in the morning if she's still coughing. David is going to take me to work and there is plenty of room for you and the baby. There's a really good children's doctor and I know he can see Mary. If she needs medicine he can give you the best remedy. You'll feel so much better once you know it is just a cough, not Tuberculosis."

Molly's words tempted Rosanna to say yes, but then she remembered James and Earl were not going to be home. "I'd like to do that, but James and Earl are going to the mainland early tomorrow morning. There would be no one here to watch the children."

"My mother would love to come over and take care of them. They're like grandchildren to her. I'll ask her as soon as I go home." Molly was confident her mother would gladly watch the Steele children. She loved the little ones and, as of yet, had no grandchildren of her own. Molly was going to be married soon and her mother was hoping she would soon have a grandchild the following year. Molly's gift of persuasion convinced Rosanna to take Mary for a check up on Saturday.

"Well, I'd better get back to my house. I still have some ironing to do. Can you believe I've waited until the hottest part of the day to do the hottest of my chores? Sometimes Me thinks I have a few loose screws in my head." Molly laughed as she got up to leave.

"Oh, wait a minute. What time would I get home?" Rosanna asked. "I need to be back in time to get dinner ready."

"There's nothing to worry about. There will be no problem finding a way home for you. There is always someone coming and going from the hospital. I know I can find transportation for you without any problem," Mary said. "Oh, how I wish I had done my ironing earlier this morning. I know it's only a few degrees cooler then, but it seems to make a difference. I just might melt! What a mess that would be!" Molly laughed at herself again as she went down the front steps, patting her hips, an indication it truly would be a sizable mess if she did melt. She was a slightly plump young woman, but it only added to her charm. She carried it well and every ounce was filled with joy and a personality that made people like her the minute they met her.

Rosanna couldn't help but smile at Molly's vivid description. She called out to her friend, "Well, if you do melt you can count on me to clean up the mess. I'll come over with my mop and bucket."

Molly couldn't help but let out a good, unexpected laugh at Rosanna's attempt at humor. Molly took this as a sign Rosanna's worry had lessened slightly. It was rare for Rosanna to joke about anything. She was normally very stoic, serious and rarely smiled. When she did smile it was usually accompanied by a deep, hearty laugh that brightened her entire face. Molly was sure this had been one of the reasons James had fallen in love with Rosanna.

Unfortunately, Rosanna's jovial mood didn't last through the day. That night as she and James were getting ready for bed she brought up her concern about Mary's coughing spells which had increased since waking up from her nap. Rosanna sat on her side of the bed, braiding her hair. James was sitting in bed reading. He was wanting to put out the light, but sensed Rosanna had something on her mind and wanted to talk. He knew the subject would be about Mary. They hadn't discussed the baby's cough in front of the other children, especially wanting to keep the subject from Junieta and Elgiva. In their young life, there was no such thing as a 'slight cough'. *Funny thing*, thought James, *how many times that phrase had been used over the years.* Like Rosanna, he'd lost count."

Rosanna finally broke the silence. "Molly came over today. I mentioned to her about our concern about Mary's cough. She suggested I go with her to the hospital tomorrow morning and have the doctor take a look at Mary. There is a doctor there that is especially good with children. It would be just as a precaution, just to ease my mind—-and yours."

"It sounds like a good idea, but what about our doctor? What about the other children? Who would stay with them? I know you haven't forgotten that Earl and I are leaving for the mainland in the morning——and how will you get there?"

"James, dear, if you'll stop to take a breath I can answer your questions." Rosanna said, right as James inhaled, getting ready to ask another question. "This doctor is a specialist for children. Molly's mother is going to watch the other children. David, you know Molly's betrothed, can take us when he drives Molly to the hospital. She has the early shift tomorrow. If all goes well, Mary and I should be home long before you and Earl get home. I'll have dinner ready and hopefully good news about Mary."

"You don't think I need to be there with you?" James' last question for the night.

"Of course I'd like you to go, but it isn't necessary this time. It is such short notice and you can't change your plans at the last minute." Rosanna tried to sound optimistic. "I'm sure it's nothing, just want to be sure. Molly will be near by if I need anything. We'll be fine." Rosanna took off her house shoes and slipped under the sheets, plumping up her pillow before she laid her head on its soft surface. Such a little luxury, clean sheets and a soft pillow were like heaven to her, but right now she didn't feel like she was living in heaven. She just prayed it wasn't going to turn out to be 'hell' if the news tomorrow was bad. They had had so much bad news in the past.

The husband and wife lay side by side, and there it was, as so many times in the past, their silence. Each one lost in their own thoughts, each afraid to express those thoughts, whether the crisis was real or perceived. It was difficult for the couple to discuss the problem at such a time. It was as if they merely talked about the subject it made it more real, more terrible. So they completely avoided talking about it, for the time being. With James, his thoughts were always on Rosanna and the children. He chose to keep his thoughts to himself. He feared the spoken word would give credence to their concerns. He was the head of the family. He had to be strong. He wanted to reach over and pull Rosanna to him, hold her in his arms, but he was afraid if he did that, he would crumble, maybe even cry. He would be useless to her if that happened. *He had to be strong,* he kept repeating to himself. It was his duty. The family leaned on his strength.

In Rosanna's mind, she felt so alone, so lost. She knew James cared and loved her, but for some reason he never took her in his arms to just hold her, to comfort her, wipe away her tears. She thought that must be one of the differences between men and women. Men were much more reserved about demonstrating their emotions. So, Rosanna was left alone to her thoughts and fears.

That night Rosanna laid on her side of the bed. She closed her eyes, but sleep was slow in coming to her. The lump in her throat kept her from breathing comfortably. The pounding of her heart seemed to be a loud, repetitive drumbeat, 'ConSUMPTION, ConSUMPTION, ConSUMPTION. At some point she realized the loud sound wasn't just her heart. The wind was making an awful sound. She hadn't paid any attention to the weather before going to bed. There had been word of a tropical storm expected to hit the island sometime in the next few days. There was no cause to be alarmed. Tropical storms were part of life on the island. That Friday night had been beautiful and there was a light breeze that brought with it the hope that cooler weather was coming.

Her main concern was she didn't want anything to interfere with tomorrow's plans to see the doctor. She felt she had offended James by not waiting until he could go with her. The subject had come to an abrupt end. She turned her head to look at her sleeping husband. He always seemed to be able to sleep regardless of what was happening to his family. He had the wonderful capacity to not worry over that which he could not control. She, on the other hand worried over everything. She knew it was a selfish thought, but she sometimes wished he would at least stay awake and keep her company during her moments of anxiety. If he ever did, it wasn't going to be tonight. Yes, tonight she was alone with her thoughts.

It was miserable just lying there and letting her thoughts run wild. If she wasn't careful, her mind would lead her down a dark path. *Mary would have Tuberculosis and being* so *little she wouldn't survive it. They would be burying their baby girl, another* victim of 'Captain Death'. *Stop it,* Rosanna shouted at herself. *This is ridiculous. It really is a slight cough. We haven't even seen the doctor yet and I'm putting her in a* grave, Rosanna kept telling herself. She decided to get out of bed. She slowly slipped out of bed, barely ruffling the covers. Putting on her robe and slippers, she tiptoed out of the bedroom. She couldn't help but chuckle to herself, at her great effort to not wake up James, the man who could sleep through anything. She went to the kitchen and filled the tea kettle with water. A good cup of tea would help relax her. She lit the stove and put the kettle on to boil. Tonight she decided to use one of her favorite china cups and saucer. She didn't have very many, but it was always a treat to use them. There was something in the sound of the cup being placed in its saucer that she couldn't explain, but it was a special sound. Maybe the soft clink as the cup rested in its saucer brought a semblance of tradition, of civility, of comfort that helped calm her. Perhaps it brought to her mind the sweet memories she had of having tea with her mother and sister a lifetime ago.

While she waited for the water to boil, she went to get her Bible out of its hiding place. Reading it also helped calm her and give her strength. She regretted she didn't yet have the courage to tell James about her secret. She was waiting for the right time. Her conscience wasn't going to let her wait much longer. Perhaps he wouldn't be so opposed to it if she shared with him how she felt so much closer to God. God was real to her. More than anything, she was convinced God loved her and no matter what happened in life, He was always going to be with her. Hadn't He proved it? She was in awe at the thought of what God's Son did to prove his love; He died for her sins and arose from the grave to give eternal life for anyone who loved and trusted in him. She wanted to share this new revelation with her husband, but didn't want any conflict to come between them. He was just as convinced there was no God as she was convinced God did exist.

She heard the water come to a boil and made herself a cup of tea. She sat down at the kitchen table, stirred a little sugar in the tea, opened her Bible and started to read. She would have been in total peace except for the noisome wind. *Oh, please God, let us get to the doctor safely tomorrow and let James and Earl have a safe trip. Bring us all safely together tomorrow night,* Rosanna softly prayed. She continued to sip her tea and read her Bible. A welcome peace washed over her. She was no longer bothered by the wind. Rosanna went back to bed, but did not fall asleep. Though she felt better, there was something deep within her that would not leave her alone, a feeling she couldn't explain. So she laid in bed listening to the wind. From its sound she knew it was coming from the North. She thought to herself, *Maybe a cool spell is here. That would be a blessed relief.*

Chapter 7

I

While most of the city slept, there was another house where another person could not sleep. It was for a similar reason, but while Rosanna could not know why she had a strange feeling that was a mystery to her, the other sleepless person knew his reason for concern. His name was Joseph Cline, brother and assistant to Galveston's chief weather forecaster, Isaac Cline.

Earlier that day, the National Weather Bureau in Washington, D.C. had sent a message to Isaac, forecasting an imminent storm was due to hit Galveston. It read, 'high winds and heavy rain'. There was no cause for alarm. The people of Galveston were accustomed to tropical storms. Every one accepted it was a way of life on the island.

Relying on Isaac's professional opinion, that Galveston was not geographically susceptible to any dangerous threat of damaging storms, most of the residents felt safe and secure. They were not bothered by the increasing winds and higher surf swells that were developing Friday evening; that is except for Joseph and a few other Galvestonians. Joseph couldn't sleep late Friday night. He was up, pacing the floor, listening to the wind and the waves as they broke on the shore. He lived with his brother and his family. The home was only a few blocks from the shore. Jospeh was convinced something very different was happening. He couldn't pin point that difference, but knew it had to do with what was happening outside. His older brother, Isaac did not agree with him. Although Isaac also had been awakened at midnight by the reverberating sounds that shook the home, he didn't think there was any cause for alarm. He realized the sound was different from any he had ever heard in his eleven years living on the island, but he had no trouble going back to sleep. His logical, scientific mind rested in the assurance that the weather bureau issued no serious warning about a dangerous storm. Sleep came easily to him, until he was awakened again at 4:00 A.M. This time by his brother.

"Isaac, you must wake up ! I know there's something very wrong."

The older brother got out of bed reluctantly and pushed Joseph out of the bedroom and took him to the parlor. He was trying to avoid waking his wife, Cora May. She was expecting their fourth child and was experiencing difficulty; it was important she get enough rest.

Joseph continued voicing his concerns to Isaac. "I can't explain exactly, but there is something happening out there. The timing of the waves is different. They're making a different sound. Call it what you want, but I feel like something horrible is going to happen."

Isaac shook his head, thinking his brother had either become over confident in his work at the bureau or he was having a breakdown of some sort. He was bordering on the brink of hysteria.

"Why do you doubt me when I tell you there is nothing to worry about?" said Isaac. "I've built this house to withstand the worst of any tropical storm that hits us. We'll never experience any dangerous storm, and even if that were possible, the bureau would alert us and it hasn't ! We've raised the storm warning flag. There's nothing else to do right now. Now go back to bed, Get some sleep. That's what I'm going to do."

Isaac turned to go back to his room. Jospeh rushed around him and blocked his way.

"You've got to listen to me. Think of Cora May and the girls. Think of all those people that depend on us, especially you. There is danger coming!"

Now Isaac was angry. He had lost all patience with his brother.

"Who do you think you are, Jospeh? Why are you questioning me? I have the science to back me up." Then, in a kinder tone, "Joseph, you're an invaluable help to me at the bureau. You know the science of which I speak. For some reason your perceived or so called premonition is getting the best of you. Calm down and for heaven sake go get some rest. Things will look different to you in the morning light."

Neither man got any rest. Isaac wouldn't admit it, but he too was starting to think something unusual was happening. Before dawn, Isaac got up and quietly got dressed. Putting on his white jacket and Panama hat, he left the house and walked to the beach.

Standing on the shore he observed the waves, noticing they were acting in a peculiar pattern. He reached into his pocket and took out his watch. He wanted to time the breaking of the waves. He noticed a strange phenomenon, one he'd never seen in his many years as a meteorologist. It was very unusual for these waves to be this high when the wind was coming from the opposite direction. Usually, a northern wind pushing against waves coming from the south calmed the ocean, sometimes making it smooth as glass. He looked up at the sky. The clouds were a dark gray and when the sun rays shone through the clouds it turned the sky into a brilliant orange. He thought to himself, *It looks like the sky is on fire with great puffs of gray smoke quickly filling the space, erasing the brilliant shades of red, orange, and* yellow. There was an old saying that came to his mind, '*Red sky at night, sailors' delight. Red sky in the morning, sailors take warning.*' He shrugged his shoulders, then turned to go home. He wanted to check on his family before he went to the bureau. Joseph was not at the house. He probably went to the bureau and was already checking the instruments, taking readings on the current data. After breakfast Isaac kissed his wife and three daughters and started to leave. He paused at the door and turned around. "I think I'll take a couple of these to Joseph; they're his favorite," he said to Cora May. He wrapped two butter flaked biscuits in a napkin and put them in his pocket. Cora May smiled at her husband, pleased with his compliment of her cooking. She had worked hard to perfect it over the years.

Joseph was busy at the bureau, just as Isaac had expected. There was an uncomfortable silence between the two brothers. The tension from their earlier conversation was still present, thick enough to cut. Isaac walked over to Joseph and pulled out the two biscuits. "I thought you might like a little breakfast. Cora May said you left the house without eating." The tension melted away. Joseph grinned and said, "You know you just brought a little bit of heaven to me." He walked over to the stove and poured a cup of coffee. Isaac got busy reading the data Joseph had collected early that morning. He was proud of his brother's work. He had proved to be a valuable asset to Isaac. Yet, Isaac always believed his own work was superior. His pride had always been impenetrable. Now it was weakening, but he still couldn't admit he may have been wrong. In his mind he had always been right. Always! He was having great difficulty thinking that he may have been wrong to have ignored his brother's warnings. His unquestionable faith in the National Weather Bureau kept him from thinking there might be a storm more serious than the predicted tropical storm. He did admit there was something extremely unusual happening. Neither brother had any idea how unusual their day was going to be.

II

The Cuban weathermen, known for their accuracy in weather forecasting, observed that an alarming storm was moving straight for Galveston, Texas. They had no way of getting the warning to the United States Weather Bureau in Washington. A ban on any communication from Cuba had been issued by Willis Moore, head of the National Weather Bureau in Washington, D.C. The ban was issued in the middle of hurricane season.

Chapter 8

By the time James and Rosanna had awakened early Saturday morning, the wind had calmed down, but the anticipation of the coming storm could be felt. The fragrance of the coming rain permeated the air. The temperature was definitely cooler.

As Rosanna took a last glance in the mirror, she made sure her hat was securely in place. She made a mental note to get an extra blanket for Mary. The cool spell was extremely welcomed by Rosanna. It seemed to give her a surge of energy that had been absent most of the summer.

She, James and Earl had had an early breakfast. There was extra coffee in the pot for Molly's mother who would be arriving soon. James and Earl had already said their goodbyes and were on their way to catch the early train. Rosanna had just enough time to check on her sleeping children.

She quietly walked into their room and made sure they were well covered. Junieta and Elgiva shared a bed, the boys shared the other one. Junieta was on her back, mouth slightly opened, sleeping soundly. Rosanna gave her a soft kiss on her cheek, then walked to the other side of the bed to give a goodby kiss to Elgiva. As she did so, Elgiva whispered, "Mama," but never opened her eyes. She turned over on her side and continued to sleep.

Rosanna then went over to the other bed to kiss her little boys goodby. They didn't stir a muscle as she kissed each child on the forehead. They looked like little angels while sleeping. No one would ever guess the scrapes and messes they could get in when awake.

She left the room, but stopped to look back at the children. She missed them already and hadn't even left the house. She was going to be gone only a few hours. *This is ridiculous,* she told herself. She determined her tender feelings were heightened because she had never left them so early in the day and had never been separated from them for more than an hour at the most. It did make the schedule easier to leave while they were asleep, but she missed the hugs and kisses and chaos they showered on her when she did leave during their waking hours. She was consoled by reminding herself she had spent a good amount of time last night talking with them, reading an extra story and singing their favorite songs, before giving them their good night hugs and kisses. They had had such a good time, she was a little worried they might want this to become an established habit.

There was a soft knock at the front door. Molly and her mother had arrived. David waited in the four seated carriage parked outside at the curb. Rosanna welcomed the two women into the front room.

"I'm ready. I just have to get Mary. Mrs. Clark, there's a pot of coffee on the stove. Please help yourself. I've wrapped the lunches in a dish towel and there's plenty for you. And be sure you have some of the buttermilk pound cake. The girls helped me make it."

Mrs. Clark smiled, "Thank you. We'll be just fine. Don't worry about a thing. I brought some things to do in case the rain keeps us indoors today. I certainly can't complain about this cooler weather."

"Nor can I. I'll be right back. Just need to get Mary and her things."

Molly said, "I'll give you a hand." She followed Rosanna to the only other bedroom in the house. Mary's crib was set right next to Rosanna and James's bed. Molly thought to herself, *Yes, this family does need more room. They're about to bust out of this little house.*

Rosanna spread a soft baby blanket on the bed and went over to the crib. She bent over her baby and gently lifted her out of the crib, placing Mary on the blanket, expertly wrapping her 'as snug as a bug in a rug'. Rosanna smiled as she thought how much the other children loved the silly little saying.

The two women left the house. David greeted Rosanna and helped the ladies get settled in the carriage. As they pulled away from the house, Rosanna looked over her shoulder and gave it a quick glance. It was a very plain little house, looked like all the other houses on the street. Yet, the lamplight shining through the window, and the breeze gently rustling the curtains made it look beautiful, cozy to her. She was at peace knowing her other four children were sleeping and Mrs. Clarke would take good care of them. Yet, she had to admit she was already anxious to return home, sit down at the dinner table, and be surrounded by the entire family. Hopefully, the day would go quickly as it usually did when one was very busy. And most of all, she would return home with the good news that Mary had a little cold, nothing more serious. She was determined to think positively.

Chapter 9

I

James and Earl were almost to the mainland. The short train trip was going smoothly. There was little conversation between the father and son as they traveled to Houston. Each one was deep in his own thoughts.

James' emotions were at a tug of war. One moment he was feeling somewhat guilty about not going with Rosanna to baby Mary's doctor's appointment. That morning at breakfast he was on the brink of cancelling his trip to the mainland and go to the hospital with Rosanna and Mary. Then he would tell himself it was just an appointment. Mary was not seriously ill; she wasn't being admitted to the hospital as a patient. At that moment he was convinced his trip to Houston was the right choice. James would always feel a sense of loyalty and indebtedness to Mr. Jenkins because he was the first person to give him a job when he had first arrived in Galveston. The Steele family had come to the city not knowing a living soul. It was a totally different atmosphere, geographically and socially from anything they had ever known. Thanks to the son of their former neighbor, Mrs. Cox, they at least had the name of Mr. Jenkins as a contact. During his five years in Galveston, James had been able to work part time at the General Store. It was an ideal situation for a school teacher who had weekends and summers free. Yes, James thought to himself, he owed a lot to Mr. Jenkins. It also helped that James was getting paid for his time making this trip.

The 'favor' he was now doing was to go to Houston to pick up a special order that missed the Friday delivery date. The customer was anxious to complete an important contract job and couldn't proceed forward until he had the parts that were still in Houston and not in Galveston. Waiting until the next Monday or Tuesday would cost him time and time was money. It was a great favor for James to go personally on Saturday to get the important order, thereby avoiding any long delays for their customer. It also left Mr. Jenkins free to work at his store on Saturday, which was his busiest day of the week.

When James knew he was going to make this day trip, he decided to take Earl with him. He reasoned it would be good for he and Earl to spend time together. James was still feeling badly about his sharpness with Earl the week before. He had never been so angry with his son. It had really affected Earl to the degree he avoided his father as much as possible. He was hurt, but also confused. It was so out of character for his father to be so stern. Earl felt like he was walking on egg shells, afraid he might do something to upset his father again. What the young boy didn't realize was that his irresponsibility, not doing his chores and being late to dinner, was out of character for him. This frightened his father. The fright turned to anger. He didn't want Earl to head down a wrong path. He was so vulnerable to the cruelty of others because of his bad leg.

As father and son sat next to each other on the train, though talking very little, James hoped their relationship would soon be back on good terms. Earl knew his father loved him. It was encouraging that there seemed to be an air of happiness about taking this trip together. Earl was glad his father had asked him to go. This was not the only thought occupying Earl's mind. He was thinking about how he could next get to the beach to meet Will. They had planned to meet the previous afternoon. Those plans fell through because James needed help to get ready for this trip. Most of Saturday's chores needed to be done on Friday. Getting messages to each other would be a challenge between the friends, so they basically agreed to meet at a certain time on certain days, (usually Fridays and Saturdays) and if one or the other didn't show up it meant something else had happened. This arrangement was brand new and this was going to be the first time to try it. It proved to be a good plan, less stressful. Earl knew Will would know something had happened to prevent their meeting. They'd try again next week.

The train slowly pulled into the station, blowing its whistle as it did so. It came to a jerky stop. Passengers prepared to get off and make their way to the day's activities. James put on his hat and placed a hand on Earl's shoulder. "Let's go get our business done, then have a good lunch before heading home. How does that sound?"

Earl thought it sounded great. He couldn't ever remember eating a meal in a restaurant or ever having had a meal where it was just he and his father.

It had the effect on Earl that James hoped it would. Earl felt for the first time he was no longer a child. His father treated him like he was a grown up, not a little boy. Earl was very short for his age, but that Saturday morning, September 8, 1900, he felt ten feet tall.

II

James' business took longer than he expected. He had to carefully make sure the invoice matched the order; wanted to make sure nothing was missing. Earl turned out to be a big help for his father doing these tabulations. Then James personally supervised the order, having it scheduled and loaded on the same train he and Earl would be taking back to Galveston.

When James was satisfied all was in order, he and Earl headed to a highly recommended restaurant-boarding house.

"This place better be as good as people say it is. It has a reputation for having 'a good home cooked meal'. We'll see if it compares with your mother's cooking," James told Earl.

"Did I hear it is close to the train depot?" Earl asked.

"Fortunately, it is. I'm so hungry I could eat a horse."

Although they were having lunch later than expected, they still had plenty of time before having to catch the afternoon train for home.

An hour later James said, "I'm so full now, I doubt I'll want much dinner when we get home. Hope your mother doesn't go to a lot of trouble getting dinner ready for us. I guess it depends what time she gets home from the doctor's appointment."

Earl nodded in agreement, "Me, too." He was so full he thought he was going to burst.

The walk to the train depot was to have been an ordinarily short distance. This afternoon it seemed as if all Houston was trying to get to the same destination. It had taken over an hour to get there. They were re-routed by a police officer twice due to the crowds clogging the regular route.

There was an unusually large crowd gathered at the train station when James and Earl finally arrived an hour later. James found it strange that the crowd was so quiet, a very eery kind of quiet. Earl noticed it also and said, "Wonder what's going on?"

"There's an empty seat over there," James said, pointing to a stool in the corner of the terminal waiting room. "You go take a load off your feet. I'll see what I can find out." James slowly edged his way to the ticket window where he hoped to get some information. He was wondering if perhaps there was a mechanical problem with the train; or maybe the tracks had to be cleared of debris or livestock, a common problem. He actually had no idea what was happening to cause the problem or what he might find out from the ticket clerk.

Several minutes later he finally reached the ticket window. "Good afternoon," James said to the man behind the counter. "Could you tell me if the 4:15 to Galveston is running on time?"

The clerk said, "All I can tell you is we haven't had any communication from Galveston for quite sometime now. Had to send a relief train from earlier this afternoon. There was some trouble with the tracks, a section had been washed out due to the storm. That's probably what is wrong with the lines, down because of the storm."

"Well, I know that wires go down often, but aren't they usually fixed in short order? It's almost four o'clock now and you're saying they're still down?" James couldn't hide his concern.

"Yes, that's what I'm saying. To be honest, it has some of us pretty worried. You have any family on the island?"

"I do. A wife and five children," James answered.

The clerk tried to look busy so he wouldn't have to say anything else. He did offer a poor attempt of trying to keep this father who was standing before him from worrying too much, "Well, I wouldn't be too worried. Nothing real bad could've happened on the island. It's never had a serious storm."

"Thank you, I hope you're right," James said. He wanted to add, "You don't sound very convincing, mister," but he kept this last part to himself. He made his way to where Earl was sitting.

Seeing his father, Earl quickly jumped up, practically knocking over the stool. "Did you find out anything?"

"No, just the wires are down and hopefully they'll be fixed soon. It happens all the time." That's all James chose to share with Earl at this time. There wasn't any sense having his young son take on a worry too heavy to hold, especially when James himself didn't know very much. He did know something very wrong was happening, but a mystery to everyone not on the island. The 'not knowing' was almost unbearable.

James nodded toward the exit and said to his son, "Let's get out of here. I need some air. All we can do for now is wait." They went outside to get away from the seemingly crushing crowd. They found an available bench around the corner of the depot.

It wasn't long before the crowd spilled out of the depot and soon surrounded James and Earl. People were starting to speculate on possibilities for the long silence, the lack of communication from Galveston. Someone had mentioned a storm had hit the island and that was why there was no communication getting to the mainland; at least not to the general public. Some were wondering if the National Weather Bureau knew anything.

Earl repositioned himself on the hard, wooden bench. He was getting very stiff and his leg was throbbing from the earlier long walk, due to the detours. He felt badly that he didn't do the gentlemanly thing and offer his place to one of the many ladies, standing, waiting in the heat. He knew if he gave up his seat, his leg couldn't bear the weight and he'd collapse. His body didn't have the physical strength to do what his conscience tried to dictate. His father had given his place to an elderly lady who appeared to be more worried than Earl and his father combined.

As James had helped the lady sit down, he tried to give her a word of encouragement, "Are you waiting for the train to Galveston?"

The lady replied, "Yes, I am."

"I'm sure we'll hear something soon. They're probably short-handed on the weekends and it takes longer to fix the wires."

The lady raised her face to give a grateful smile to James. "I'm sure you are right," she said. James almost believed her, but her eyes said something else, She couldn't tell him that something deep inside her led her to believe that something very terrible was happening in Galveston. There was nothing anyone could do but wait and pray.

Chapter 10

That Saturday morning in Galveston could be described as experiencing a pleasant change in the weather. The northerly wind brought cooler weather, cool enough in the early hours to need a jacket or shawl if venturing out doors.

Few residents were aware that at 7:00 that morning the water from the gulf was invading the city in spite of the strong winds from the north.

Molly, Rosanna and baby Mary had reached the hospital without any difficulty. Getting out of the blustery wind and entering the warmth of the hospital's shelter felt good. Molly led Rosanna to a small room where she could tend to Mary's needs while waiting to see the doctor.

"I'll be back in a few minutes. I need to check my patients' charts. Would you like a good, hot cup of coffee?"

"That would be wonderful. In the meantime I'll feed Mary. She's been so patient," Rosanna said.

"Oh, good. I'll be back as soon as I can." Molly left the room. Rosanna rearranged Mary's blankets. She then held her baby close and enjoyed a mother's delight as her child contentedly fell asleep in her arms. Rosanna never tired of watching the precious positions a baby found to do with their tiny hands. This was her sixth child, and the wonder was as special as it was with the first. Mary first laid her little hand on Rosanna's chest, then she moved it to her own little cheek. One of Rosanna's favorite positions was when the tiny hand formed a fist, placed directly under the tiny chin, as if Mary was deep in thought while she slept.

Molly was true to her word. She returned in a short time with the cup of coffee she had promised her friend. "I was able to speak with the doctor I told you about. He'll be able to see Mary sometime after lunch. In the meantime, I can put her in a crib to finish her nap. When she wakes up I can get her ready for the doctor's exam. There'll be plenty of time for the both of you to have lunch."

"May I come with you?" Rosanna asked.

"In a little while you can join us. Right now I'm going to place the crib right next to my desk. I'll keep a good eye on her. You're not to worry, You'll be much more comfortable staying here." Molly said. "May I get anything else for you?"

"Thank you, no. I'll be fine. I brought some knitting to do while waiting." Rosanna said.

For the second time, Molly left Rosanna, but this time Rosanna was all alone. It was a strange feeling for the wife and mother of six children. She couldn't remember ever being totally alone. She was sure it had been many years ago. Instead of knitting, she decided to read her Bible which she had put in the small bag with her knitting needles and yarn. It was still her secret, but today, in the hospital, she didn't feel nearly as guilty as she did when she was home.

She opened the Bible, ready to read, but she first said a quick prayer asking God to keep her family safe. She couldn't help but wonder how Mrs. Clarke was doing with the children, especially Roy and Albert. She knew the girls would not be a problem. She couldn't say the same about the boys. They were normal, active, adventuresome little boys. Albert wanted to do everything Roy did; go everywhere Roy went. Roy was not a mischievous little boy, but he did like to explore and experiment. Thus, two little boys were always on the move except when sleeping.

Chapter 11

Mrs. Clarke was doing just fine; the morning went very well. Junieta and Elgiva were wonderful helpers. After breakfast, they all sat on the front porch and watched the water from the bay start to invade the neighborhood's front lawns, delighting many of the children who squealed, splashed and played in the water. They were having as much fun as they did when they went to the beach, but today it was as if the beach had come to them. Roy begged to play in the water. Mrs. Clarke knew if she said 'yes' to his pleas, Albert would automatically try to follow Roy. Such a situation could, would get out of hand quickly. She also knew the girls longed to play in the water. It showed in their faces and their eyes lit up at the very mention of the idea. But today would be too risky. The wind and cooler weather was not a good combination for the sake of their health.

Mrs. Clarke sadly had to say, "Not today dear little ones. But I have an idea." Mrs. Clarke quickly offered an alternative. "Junieta, I need you and Elgiva to get some paper and pencils for us. Any thing else you can think of for color, maybe some fabric scraps or ribbon." The girls quickly did as asked and disappeared in to the house, and just as quickly, returned to the porch with all requested items in their hands.

"This is what we're going to do," Mrs. Clarke said, happy to see the excitement on the faces of her charges.

Thirty minutes later she was helping the children to launch their decorated paper boats in the water, being very careful that no one fell from the steps in to the water which would have defeated her purpose for making the boats. The children laughed and giggled as they watched their little fragile vessels go in all directions, wherever the water took them. Suddenly Roy let out a loud, "Oh NO " as he watched his boat tip over and disappear in the water. He was about to try to save his boat and lunged for the water. Elgiva quickly grabbed at her little brother and luckily caught the edge of his shirt, saving him from completing his 'watery rescue'. Mrs. Clarke caught Albert in time before he tried to follow his brother. Albert did not like being confined in the arms that kept him away from his older brother and when he looked at his brother's sad expression, he thought he had a good reason to cry. Mrs. Clarke quickly consoled the little boys by helping them make another boat, but cautioning them that when all the boats were gone, whether they sailed out of view or sank, they would have to go indoors. It was soon going to be time for lunch and then a nap.

"Let's find some fish to eat for lunch. They're in the water with our boats, right, Mrs. Clarke?" Roy didn't want to leave the water.

"Maybe we'll go fishing another day, Roy. Your mother already made lunch for us. We'll eat, then get ready for a nap. Since you've been so good today, I'll read your favorite story. Would you like that?" Mrs. Clarke asked. Junieta looked over at her sister and shrugged her shoulders, raised her eyebrows, signaling she was puzzled by Mrs. Clarke's statement that Roy had been 'so good today'. Elgiva agreed with Junieta's opinion, but they were not the ones in charge. It was not their place to question their elders.

In answer to Mrs. Clarke's suggestion, Roy nodded his head, but not with much enthusiasm. He took hold of Mrs. Clarke's outreached hand. Albert was straddling Mrs. Clarke's hip, wriggling, trying to get down and hold her other hand, just like Roy was doing. He was practically his brother's shadow.

"Settle down, you little monkey. I'll let you down as soon as we get in the house. Junieta, would you hold open the door for us, please?" said Mrs. Clarke. As she passed Junieta, the big sister couldn't help but tickle Albert, thinking it would distract him for the thirty seconds it took to get in the house. It worked, but it was a miracle Mrs. Clarke didn't drop him. With a bit of huffing and puffing from the exertion, Mrs. Clarke set the toddler down on the floor, relieved when his two feet were solidly on the floor. It had almost been his head.

An hour later lunch was finished and the boys were in bed, napping soundly after a full morning of fun and physical activity. Junieta was quietly reading, totally absorbed in her favorite book. Elgiva was happy playing with her paper dolls. For the moment, Mrs. Clarke was content sitting in the only rocking chair in the home. She was gently rocking, her hands were folded in her lap, either resting or perhaps praying. Her eyes were closed, either napping or praying. It wasn't long before she was letting out a soft whistle of a snore. She was napping. The sound caught Elgiva's attention. She looked up from her dolls and glanced at Mrs. Clarke. She whispered to Junieta, "Look at Mrs. Clarke; she's sound asleep. Isn't she a cute old lady?"

"It's nicer to say 'elderly lady' not 'old lady', Junieta smiled at her little sister." I guess she's not use to taking care of four children."

"Guess not. I sure do like her," said Elgiva. "I wonder when Mama and Baby Mary will be home?"

"They'll probably be here shortly before dinner," said Mrs. Clarke.

Both girls jerked to attention and looked back at Mrs. Clarke. Her eyes were still closed, but she had a definite smile on her face after surprising the girls with her answer. The girls shrugged their shoulders, both wondering how much Mrs. Clarke had heard. They were so hoping she hadn't heard the 'old lady' part.

Chapter 12

While the children of Galveston were taking their afternoon nap and business men were finishing their long, leisurely lunch, there was a group of people gathered at the beach to watch the impressive waves breaking on the white sand. The bay was also providing a source of amazement as the northern, gusty winds pushed the waters in to the streets and neighborhood yards. The sky was darkening. The heavy, swollen gray clouds were beginning to empty their load of water and rain began to fall on Galveston, forcing the residents to seek shelter. The tropical storm had arrived. These storms always brought an element of excitement to the islanders and tourists. Such storms caused more inconvenience than fear.

One of the earliest inconveniences was the street cars were unable to operate by 12:30 P.M. Intended passengers had to walk, and in many places, wade through the rising water to get to their destination. The rain was quickly adding to the water from the bay and the gulf, causing flooding in many areas of the city. Great gusts of wind were becoming more frequent and stronger.

Isaac and Joseph Cline were being kept busy at the weather station in the Levi building, carefully observing the weather pattern and calculating data. An earlier report from the Washington headquarters said the tropical storm was heading east and north, totally bypassing the Gulf of Mexico.

The storm took the two weathermen by surprise when it was definitely heading for Galveston. By 2:30 P.M., Isaac realized the storm was going to be much worse than originally reported. Joseph was not surprised, but said nothing. Isaac wrote a cable to Willis Moore, head of the Weather Bureau based in Washington, D.C.. He sent Joseph to Western Union to deliver the cable. Isaac then decided to go home to get something to eat and check on his family. He still felt there was no cause for alarm at this time. He was confident his home would be more than sufficient to weather the storm. He had gone to extra care and expense to build a house that would be a fortress against any storm that would hit Galveston.

Joseph went to Western Union to telegraph Isaac's message. The cable was unable to be sent because all the wires were down. There was one other way to get the message to Washington. Joseph thought it was worth a try. It was difficult, but Joseph finally sent the message by telephone. Having completed his mission, Joseph headed for home. By then it was a difficult journey. The water was waist deep, making progress extremely slow. He arrived at the house by 5:30. The house was crowded with other people trying to find shelter from the ever growing, stronger storm. The Cline house had a reputation for being one of the best built homes in the city.

Chapter 13

I

The afternoon had not gone well at the hospital. The John Sealy Hospital was located near the bay. It was receiving the full blast of the blustering wind gusts coming from the North. It was as if the bay was a great basin of water being poured out on the land.

Molly was busy organizing her patients, getting them ready to be transferred to the upper floor, since the lower floor was quickly becoming flooded. Fortunately, she was able to delegate most of the instructions from her desk. Baby Mary was miraculously sleeping through the raised voices and aids rushing to get people and equipment moved. Molly had sent a message to Rosanna to go to the second floor where she and Mary would meet her there as soon as possible.

The wind that battered the building struck fear in Molly's heart. She sat down at her desk to finish a letter she had started earlier in the day, asking David to come get them to a safer place. She had to get it delivered while there was still a chance of finding an errand boy to take it. Then she would take Mary to the second floor. The water was rising rapidly and it wouldn't be long before the first floor would be flooded.

As she wrote, she prayed that the letter would reach David in time to rescue Rosanna, Mary and herself. She dipped her pen in the ink well and with difficulty, tried to steady her hand as she wrote:

A.M.

'It does not require a great stretch of imagination
this structure a shaky old boat at sea. The whole
thing rocking like a reef, surrounded by water, said
water growing closer, ever closer. Have my hands
full quieting nervous, hysterical women.

12-noon

Things beginning to look serious. Water up to the
first floor in the house, all over the basement of the
hospital. Cornices, roofs window lights blinds flying
in all directions.
The scenes about here are distressing. Every
thing washed away. Poor people trying to save their
bedding, & clothing. Me thinks the poor nurses will be
trying to save their beds in short order. Now flames in
the distance. It is all a grand, fine sight. Our beautiful
Bay, a raging torrent.

Baby Mary woke up crying. It was past her feeding time. There was no way Molly could take her to her mother at this moment. She picked up the small bundle and soothed the hungry baby as she went to a cabinet where there was a small supply of prepared baby bottles, ready for infants unable to be fed by their mother for various reasons. Molly prayed this would work for Mary. Taking the baby back to her crib, Molly was successful in propping Mary in a comfortable position with a rolled blanket supporting her back which kept her from rolling on to her back. With one hand Molly fed the baby while with the other hand she wrote her letter, desperate to finish it. She looked down at Mary, "Sorry, little one. I wish I could hold you properly. I'd love to cuddle you in my arms and feed you, sing a song to you. I'm even sorrier I can't take you to your Mama right now. As soon as I find someone to deliver my letter, I'll take you to her. It'll be in just a minute."

Molly couldn't help but think how frightening this must be for Rosanna. She must be frantic to have her baby with her.

Molly's nervousness was growing with the increasing seriousness of their situation. She was overwhelmed getting patients and as many hospital supplies and equipment moved to the upper floor; doing all this while keeping Mary close to her. Molly had no idea where Rosanna was. She was suppose to be on the second floor, but there was a lot of square footage to cover, long hallways with numerous rooms. She had to get mother and child together! She didn't trust anyone to perform such a task. She instructed the first available nurse, "Please go get Mrs. Steele and bring her to me. She is supposed to be on the second floor, where exactly I'm not sure. I'm making my way to the second floor as soon as I can. We're running out of time; the first floor is flooding quickly. When you find Mrs. Steele bring her to the nurses' station, Section 140 B I'll be there. Please hurry! It's important you find her—SOON!"

It was now the afternoon. She had to finish her letter. Too many responsibilities had interrupted her efforts to send for help. She was relieved that Mary now slept peacefully. Molly would feel a lot better once this little one was back in her mother's arms. She began again to write,

3:00 P.M.

Am beginning to feel a weakening desire for something "to cling to." Should feel more comfortable in the embrace of your arms. You hold yourself in readiness to come to us? Should occasion demand?

Darkness is overwhelming us, to add to the horror. Dearest—I—reach out my hand to you, my heart—my soul.'

II

Anne, the nurse who Molly had instructed to get Mrs. Steele, found her duty much more difficult than first expected. Certain parts of the hospital were impassable.

It took several turns to get to an accessible passage. Short of breath, the young nurse felt better once she started up the stairs to the second floor. Now she had the challenge of finding Rosanna. The scene before her was one of chaos and fear. The shaking building and the rising water were causing much alarm.

The head nurse was trying to bring some semblance of order and calm. It was not an easy task to do. There had never been a situation of such seriousness to be faced in the history of the hospital. They had handled epidemics of Typhoid, Yellow Fever, Tuberculosis and other various diseases with grand competency; recruiting necessary staff-doctors and nurses, aids, kitchen staff, and janitorial help, having extra supplies ordered and ready to use. It had all worked like a "well oiled machine". At all times the building that housed the direst needs of an ailing population had stood strong. The structure protected them from all external harm. But now, this same structure was fragile under the influence of the storm. Its walls shook, its beams groaned, its windows shattered as the wind grew stronger by the minute. There was great fear that the roof over their heads might be peeled away as easily as one lifts the lid from an ordinary box.

Nurse Anne was able to ask the head nurse if she knew where a Mrs. Steele might be. "She's not a patient. She brought her baby here to be checked by the doctors. Nurse Molly brought her." Anne asked in a loud voice, trying to be heard over the storm and human commotion.

Fortunately, the Head Nurse knew of Rosanna and pointed to an adjoining hallway. Anne was encouraged and headed in that direction.

The lights in the hospital were no longer working. An occasional lantern had been lit and set on the floor of the hallway. Nurse Anne picked up one, grateful to have the light. She slowly made her way down the hall, having to scoot shattered glass out of her way. The floor was carpeted with the glass that had for a short time kept the wind and rain out of the hospital. Now the elements came through the open spaces, drenching the young nurse. Luckily the lantern continued to burn. Her progress was slow, having to also pick her way through debris and rearranged hospital furniture. It was so strange to see empty beds crowding the halls, but it did not frighten her. It gave her a sense of relief, thinking the patients had been successfully moved to a safer place.

She finally found a group of people gathered in a small room at the far end of the hall. In the limited lantern light it appeared to have suffered minor damage from the storm. She asked, practically screaming the words, "Is there a Mrs. Steele here, Rosanna Steele?"

Rosanna barely heard the young nurse's question over the noise of the storm. She wasn't sure, but she thought she heard her last name. "I'm Mrs. Steele," she shouted. "Over here," she added. She got up from her chair and edged her way to the nurse. She couldn't see her face, but recognized the uniform. She hoped it was Molly, bringing her baby to her. When she got closer to the nurse, she felt her heart melt in disappointment.

"Were you looking for a Mrs. Steele?" Rosanna asked. "That is me." Not waiting for an answer she rushed the nurse with more questions. "Is my baby alright? Where is Nurse Molly?"

"I'm Nurse Anne. Molly sent me to find you and take you to your baby. But we can't go now. We're going to have to stay here for a while. It's too difficult to try to get through the hospital right now. I'm sure it won't be long until the storm eases up. When I saw Molly and your baby, they were just fine. Mary had been fed and was sleeping like an angel. She's in good hands. Molly won't let anything happen to your baby." Nurse Anne hoped her words helped ease Rosanna's worries, but knowing how most mothers felt about their children, she doubted this mother felt much better.

Rosanna took a deep breath. Her heart had returned to its normal place, but was beating so hard it sounded as if it now resided in her ears. The thought of Mary sleeping peacefully made her feel slightly better, but she longed to hold her little baby.

The afternoon that was filled with panic, fear and worry then turned into a night of terror. Rosanna found herself huddled in the corner of the small room she had shared for hours with strangers, still on the second floor. The group was a combination of patients and hospital staff. No one had left the room and no one had entered it since Rosanna had talked with Nurse Anne.

Half the building had been in the storm's monstrous grip and was scattered among other buildings, homes and most alarming of all, among the corpses of the dead.

For hours total darkness surrounded the small group. There were occasional glimpses of what accompanied the never ending roar and screeching howls of the wind. A flash of lightening would rip through the darkness and reveal to the huddled group the absence of a large portion of the hospital. A great, empty void where only hours earlier nurses were busily buzzing around taking care of their patients; where doctors had been making their rounds, checking their patients and giving instructions to the nurses.

Rosanna was horrified by what she saw, but even more so at what she didn't see. She refused to let her thoughts dwell for long on where her baby might be. She kept telling herself, *Surely she's in a safe place. Molly wouldn't let any harm come to Mary.*

Her thoughts would then turn to her other children, trying to convince herself they were safe. They were in a different part of the city, miles from where the hospital was located. Then she would lift her eyes toward the heaven she couldn't see and asked God to please, please protect all her children. She could feel a large lump in her throat, she could barely swallow. She felt her eyes burn and fill with tears. *'No, not now!* She screamed to herself. *You cannot fall apart now. You must be strong!* she silently commanded herself. She wrapped her arms around herself, in a determined attempt to keep herself from falling apart. The familiar nursery rhyme, "Humpty Dumpty", came to her mind. She started to laugh, but not with the laughter of the joyful, but of the hysterical. She quickly clamped a hand over her mouth to prevent any sound which would betray her inner struggle to stay sane. The rhyme was so perfect of how she felt.

> 'Humpty Dumpty sat on a wall.
> Humpty Dumpty had a great fall.
> All the king's horses and all the king's men
> could not
> put Humpty Dumpty together again.'

She suddenly had great empathy for the fellow, but certainly did not want to end up like he did. She knew if she fell apart, she too, could never be put together, not by all the king's horses or all the king's men, could put Rosanna together.

Chapter 14

In many ways it was a blessing Rosanna did not know what was happening to others during the storm. There was hardly a section of the city that was not in the grips of the storm.

On the opposite side of the island, St. Mary's orphanage was facing the same monster. The two-story building where the boys lived was located practically on the beach. Just north of it was the girls' dormitory. Earlier in the day, the nuns sensed the boys could be in danger, for the Tropical Storm was growing stronger at an alarming rate. They transferred all the boys to the girls' dormitory which was a similar, but stronger building and not as close to the beach. At first, the children were excited to watch the waves grow higher as the wind gained in strength. It wasn't long before the excitement turned to fright. In an attempt to lessen the children's fear, the nuns had the ninety-three children sing an old French hymn, 'Queen of the Waves'.

It was getting close to dinner time, but no one was thinking about food. The gusting winds were nearing 100 miles per hour, at times even stronger. The Gulf waters and the water from the Bay, both slammed the island, flooding most of the city. The nuns and children heard a loud crash and watched as the boys' dormitory was destroyed into a thousand pieces. It was as if the structure had been merely twigs now being tossed, going in every direction. The nuns feared some of those 'twigs' would crash into the remaining girls' building dooming it to the same fate. They took a clothes line and cut it in to ten strips. Each nun then took eight or nine children and tied the rope to the belts which each child wore around their waist and attached the end to their own waist. The plan was to keep all the children together. It was a noble plan the brave nuns had devised, but the outcome proved disastrous. The lower floor and foundation was hit by an extraordinary rush of waves and debris. The girls' building fell, with the roof collapsing and trapping all inhabitants in the swirling, gushing, crashing water. The ropes of security became entangled in the debris of the rushing water. It was impossible to escape. All the nuns and ninety children drowned. Three older boys, who had not been attached to the rope, were able to swim to the surface, and by some miracle survived.

Chapter 15

I

What Rosanna did not know was the valiant effort Mrs. Clarke made to keep the children safe.

Their morning had gone smoothly and the children delighted in sailing their homemade paper boats and later an indoor game of hide and seek. They had lunch,and then the boys were put down for an afternoon nap. Mrs. Clarke and the girls had settled in to what they thought would be a cozy, peaceful afternoon. The morning rain had not let up, but was approaching a downpour.

"My word, it sounds like someone's throwing pebbles at the house," Mrs. Clarke said as she continued to rock in the maple rocking chair, one of the few treasures in the Steele's home decor. She never missed a stitch in her knitting project.

"It does seem extra loud," Junieta replied. "I'm surprised Roy and Albert haven't woken up yet."

Elgiva took a role in the conversation, "You know what Mama always says, 'A train could come barreling through the house and the boys would sleep through the noise and never move a muscle.'"

Mrs. Clarke chuckled, "Is that so? Not me. I'm such a light sleeper, a cat tip toeing through the room could wake me up—I think most mothers are that way. It's built in to us."

The girls enjoyed listening to Mrs. Clarke, whether she was telling a story or just chatting with them like she was this afternoon, her voice was magical.

Elgiva put down her doll and walked over to the window. She was surprised to see how much the water had risen since lunch. She turned to Junieta and Mrs. Clarke. She motioned them with her hand to come to the window. "Come look at this," she said.

"My goodness, we've got a regular river running through our street," Mrs. Clarke tried to make light of the situation, but she knew it was not a laughing matter. In all her years living on the island, she had never witnessed this much water, rising this quickly. It was almost to the front door, and at this rate, would be coming in the house, which was built several feet above the ground.

Mrs. Clarke remembered hearing earlier in the day, 'Rain and high winds. A coastal storm. Nothing to worry about.' That is what the forecast had told the islanders. Everyone had gone about their normal activities. This was not one of their normal storms.

Nothing to worry about? Mrs. Clarke repeated to herself. She tried not to worry, but she had four young children to think about. They were in her care. Immediate action was needed. Above all, she had to remain calm for the sake of the children.

Moving away from the window, she took each girl by the hand and bent over to look them directly in the eye.

"I tell you what needs to be done. Junieta, I want you to gather as many towels, blankets, whatever you can find so we can roll them up and place them at the front and back doors to keep out the water for as long as we can. I'll close the windows. Elgiva I want you to start moving some of you father's books to the kitchen counter tops. We don't want them to get wet and your father come home to find his books as wet as dish rags."

Junieta grabbed her mother's favorite throw quilt off the settee and started to roll it up to put it at the front door. Mrs. Clarke saw her out of the corner of her eye just in time to rescue the quilt, "Oh, sweet girl, let's leave that until last. Hopefully, we won't need it. For now let's put it on top of the pie safe. I'll help you." Junieta smiled in agreement.

When all the windows had been closed and items of value, mainly sentimental value had been put in higher places, Mrs. Clarke told the girls, "We may all be sitting on top of each other before this storm's gone. Won't that be a sight!" She laughed and the girls caught her light-hearted mood, too young to realize it was far from being 'light'. Junieta and Elgiva felt as though they were playing a new, exciting game.

Mrs. Clarke went to the bedroom to get the boys. Roy was sitting up in bed, rubbing his eyes.

"What's happening?" he asked in a muffled voice, still not totally awake.

Mrs. Clarke scooped Albert into her arms and positioned him on her hip. She reached out for Roy and took him by the hand. She explained to him as she took the boys to the parlor,

"It's one of our Galveston storms. I've seen plenty, nothing to worry your little head. You know what we're going to do?"

She wasn't really asking a question as much as she was trying to peak Roy's curiosity and distract him from the storm.

Roy was wide eyed and answered, "What?"

"We're going to play a game. We're all going to get in this boat." She nodded toward the settee. "We're going to paddle as fast as we can to get away from Captain Jack, the fiercest pirate known in these parts."

Roy was excited at the prospect of a new adventure. He quickly scampered up to position himself in the 'boat'. He looked over the edge of both the sides of the sette, now piled with pillows, cushions and various items. Then he quickly checked behind him. Something was missing. "Where are the paddles?" he asked.

In a whisper, Mrs. Clarke asked Junieta to run to the kitchen and get the broom or mop. That was the best they could do for now.

Once everyone was situated on the settee, now 'the boat', the game began. Every time the rain pelted the house, Mrs. Clarke would say, "They're getting mighty close! We need to row faster."

Roy would tighten his grip on the paddle and lift his shoulders, then lower the paddle in to the water, which for now, was only make believe. He repeated this movement over and over again as fast as he could.

Elgiva told him, "If you get tired, Roy, I'll take over for a while." Roy never surrendered his paddle.

When the thunder boomed so loudly it shook the walls of the house, Mrs. Clarke would say, "My goodness, they're bringing out the big guns after us. That's cannon fire for sure!"

The children were so caught up in the game they didn't notice the fear in Mrs. Clarke's eyes, nor did they hear the slight quiver in her voice.

She knew from experience this storm was far from being in the Tropical Storm category. She had heard about hurricanes and the very word sent a shiver up her spine. It wasn't until the walls of the house started to bulge and the window panes shattered from the force of the wind that the children became frightened. Junieta and Elgiva screamed in unison. Little Albert started to cry. Roy sat rigid, trying hard not to cry. He bit his lower lip to try to stop it from quivering. Mrs. Clarke couldn't blame any of them for she felt the same way, but couldn't show it. She knew they must find help.

It wasn't dinner time yet, but a darkness was descending on the city. The wind was growing stronger as the hours of the day were rolling in to the night. The water from the bay was being shoved onto the land, flooding homes, buildings and anything else in its path. The waves from the Gulf were reaching unimaginable heights and strength. They looked like giant claws reaching out to gather all it could from the island and take their bounty back to the sea.

There was only one thing for Mrs. Clarke to do, get the children out of the house immediately. She had to shout for the children to hear her.

"Junieta, you and Elgiva take hold of Roy. Don't let go for anything. I've got Albert. We've got to get out of the house now! Follow me. Stay close, dear ones," she shouted.

No sooner were the words out of her mouth than the house started to tilt. The stout, strong woman and the four children reached the front door and exited the house. Mrs.

Clarke grabbed Junieta's hand and pulled the human chain to the porch railing. She had the three older children clustered in front of her, while she still held Albert tightly on her hip. They could barely see anything in front of them. The rain was like a dark, gray wall they couldn't get through, while at the same time it felt like sharp needles were being thrust at their bodies, stinging with every contact. The grand woman tried to shield the children with her body. At that moment a man saw the small group, huddled together on the tilting porch. He rushed up the steps, practically swimming to reach them. "Let me help you," he yelled over the noise of the storm. He lifted Roy with one arm and started to reach for Albert, but Mrs. Clarke said, "Take the girls. I can manage him." The man did as she said. This was no time for a discussion. Junieta and Elgiva clung to the man, holding on to his jacket. Mrs. Clarke now clutched Albert with both arms, keeping him close to her body. She followed the stranger, hopefully to a safe place. They had slowly progressed only a few yards when they heard a loud crash behind them. The Steele home had been turned upside down and broke into pieces. They had escaped just in time. *Oh God,* Mrs. Clarke whispered to herself. *Only You know what lies ahead. Give us strength. We are in your hands, dear Lord.*

The raging wind was flinging beams of wood and steel through the air like warriors of old slinging their spears, piercing anyone in its path, killing or severely wounding its victims. Tiles were being ripped from their roofs as if they were mere pages of a book being torn from its spine. Once air borne, they too became lethal weapons, having no mercy for anyone it struck.

The people of Galveston were desperately trying to survive. When not overtaken by the flooding waters, they were dodging flying objects. It wasn't unusual to see furniture flying, twirling through the air. For some people it could be a dangerous item, to others it would become a life saving raft to keep them from drowning. When not dodging the deadly objects, people were fighting the countless snakes whose homes the storm had disturbed so ferociously. Many people died from snake bites.

As terrifying as the sights and experiences were, it was the sounds the people heard that made them feel they were in a different world; a world beyond anyone's imagination. The wind, and the rushing, swirling water were so overpowering a person could hardly hear their own shouts. There was a strange sound intermingling with the storm. It was indistinguishable, deeply disturbing. It would fill the air, then get swallowed up by the storm. If one could see the faces of the desperate, struggling people, they would have a clue to the strange sound. The faces showed every sign of screaming, calling the names of their loved ones, yearning to hear an answer. But these voices were rarely heard above the storm. It was as if the ocean had released a million banshees, screaming and howling, overtaking any human sound. The torment would last through the night.

II

James and Earl were experiencing another kind of torment—-the torment of knowing something horrible could be happening to their loved ones and they were helpless. They suffered the torture of waiting.

Chapter 16

I

Sunday morning dawned a new day. If one looked to the Gulf, it was smooth and calm, not giving the slightest hint of its monstrous tantrum the previous night.

But all one had to do was look to the North and see where Galveston once stood. There was an abundance of evidence a great tragedy had occurred.

Homes and office buildings were gone. The city was laid flat. Buried and scattered among the destruction were thousands of men, women and children. Those who survived had the gruesome job of gathering as many bodies as possible and take them to a central location in hopes they might be identified by surviving family members or friends.

The task was overwhelming. With so many lost, the island was in danger of disease which could easily cause the death rate to rise.

One attempt at solving the problem was to load the bodies of the deceased, weighted with rocks, on to barges and take them out to sea for burial. The sea rebelled and delivered most of the bodies back to shore. Since there was not room nor time to bury these poor souls on land, it was decided that it would be best to burn them.

This was the scene Rosanna faced after enduring a night that rivaled the worst of nightmares. She and the people who had shared a small space on the second floor of the hospital emerged from their shelter and were transported to a safer building. Rosanna felt she was in a daze, moving in a stupor. Each step she took slowly brought her to reality. She looked all around her, wondering where was her baby? She thought, *Surely Molly's going to bring her to me any minute now. She's probably just as intent on finding me as I for her.*

No matter where she looked she never found Mary or Molly. She didn't give up hope. There were so many people needing to be helped, so much to do that she imagined Molly was somewhere giving aid to someone. Mary would surely be with her. It was just going to take time to find them.

Rosanna was determined to find a way to get home and be with her other children, make sure they were safe. She then wondered if she still had a home. As far as her eyes could see, there was destruction. House or not, that wasn't important to her now. The only thing that mattered was to find her children. Molly was sure to be worried about her mother and anxious to find her. Perhaps she was headed in the same direction as Rosanna and their paths would cross.

It seemed to Rosanna she was always hearing a voice in the far distance giving instructions to the ever moving groups of displaced people. She wasn't sure if they were talking to her or someone else. She wasn't the only one in a state of confusion. That could safely be said about the majority of the island's survivors. One moment someone was giving her a blanket.

Another moment she was being given some water and a little food. Both were scarce on the island until help could come from the mainland.

For two days Rosanna was shuffled from one location to another. On the second day she found herself standing in a line, waiting to register her name and the names of her family members and their ages who were still missing. It was a well organized effort to try to reunite families and also try to get an idea how many lives had been lost in the storm. It was a job filled with joy and sorrow. Great joy in seeing families brought back together, heartbreaking sorrow when families discovered a reunion would never take place while on this earth.

Finally, Rosanna found herself standing in front of a young woman with a kind face. "Hello. I'm Mrs. Parker. We're going to help you in any way we can. May I have your name?"

"I am Mrs. James Steele, Rosanna Steele. I'm looking for my children. There's five of them. Is there any word where they might be? Is there another kind of hold station like this one for family members that have been separated?" Rosanna could feel her throat closing on her. She started to breathe quickly, fearing she was going to run out of air. She was so nervous. She was hoping for the best, but fearing the worst.

She continued, "Excuse me. I'm here alone. My husband and oldest son went to the mainland on Saturday." She found it hard to focus on one subject at a time when a thousand things were whirling in her mind. Then she went back to the subject of finding her children. "The two oldest girls, are Junieta and Elgiva Steele." She had to pause to get hold of herself. "Then there's Roy, Albert and baby Mary." There, she had given all the names without falling apart. She continued, back on the subject of her husband and son, "Are there any people on the mainland getting across to the island? Do you think they've heard about what's happened here?"

The woman taking Rosanna's information stopped writing and looked at the woman standing across the desk from her. There was very little news she could tell, but she did her best.

"For now, only supplies and professionals are getting to the island. There's very limited transportation to and from the island since the storm. One of our railroad bridges was completely destroyed. Your family probably knows about the storm. The newspapers have been reporting about it daily throughout the country."

"They must be frantic wondering how we are!" Rosanna's voice starting to shake. "I don't even know how we are. I've got to find my children. Where do I start? Is there any way to get word to my husband?" Rosanna shook her head, answering her own question, "No. I know that's impossible. I don't know where they are on the mainland." It seemed Rosanna was constantly trying to not become a Humpty Dumpty. She stiffened her back, swallowed hard and took a deep breath to keep her composure.

Mrs. Parker, listening to her story, also had to struggle to keep her composure. She had heard countless stories and each one tore at her heart, piece by piece. She couldn't imagine how all these people felt. She and her family had, by some miracle survived the storm with minimal damage to their home and no loss of life. With a voice filled with compassion, "Let's get the ages of your children. You said there are five of them?" Rosanna nodded her head. She repeated their names and added the ages.

"This will help. There are several places like this one set up in the city. Once a day we coordinate and compare our lists. The lists are then posted for the public to read at this location. We are centrally located. If you see the names of your children on the list, we will arrange to bring them here to you. So if you"ll check the list every day, hopefully you'll soon have your children with you." Mrs. Parker paused for a moment' her next suggestion would not be an easy one to tell. "There's another list you can check. The newspapers are printing a list of the deceased who have been identified."

Rosanna interrupted her, "You mean lists of those who perished in the storm?"

"Well, yes. But even those lists are not always accurate. There are so many. For now it's good we have your name and the names of your children. That will help. Do you have any family or friends to help you?" Do you need a place to stay?

"I'm in one of the tents the city has provided."

"Good. Check back here every day. I'll also keep a check on the list and let's pray you and your children will soon be together again."

Rosanna turned to make room for the next person in line, but had another question to ask, "How will my husband find us once he gets back to the island?"

"There'll be people posted at different areas to help direct people to this holding station. Once the lines are open and the general public are allowed back on the island, it won't take long for him to find you. And you know, someone is probably taking information from your children as we speak, and we'll soon have you all together." The kind woman smiled reassuringly at

Rosanna. She felt a little worried she may be giving Rosanna false hope, but what else could she say?

Rosanna walked away, saying to herself, *I hope I can remember that woman's name.* She kept walking and tried to make her way back to her temporary home. Even if she could close her eyes to the shattered island and the dead bodies still scattered among the debris, she could not escape the horrid smell. She couldn't believe what had happened to Galveston, to her and her family and all the others.

II

Rosanna decided she needed to keep busy while waiting for news of her children. It was her way of surviving. Doing nothing would only cause her to become physically and probably mentally ill. It had been days since the storm and still she had had no word of her family. She kept busy by helping distribute clothes that had been arriving in bulk from concerned people from all over the country. When they had heard about the storm they were eager to help. Clara Barton, founder and leader of The American Red Cross had come to the island and was instrumental in getting necessary supplies to Galveston.

The weather was still extremely hot and the humidity was so thick it covered the island in a misty veil.

Rosanna had just given supplies to a family who had lost their mother in the storm. The next man in line looked at her and asked, "Excuse me, aren't you Mrs. Steele?"

She looked at the man, not immediately recognizing him. Then she gasped, "You're David, Molly's intended. Oh my word, How are you? Have you seen Molly or my baby?"

"I'm so sorry. I haven't found Molly or Mary yet. Mrs. Steele, it doesn't look good. Word has it they may have been caught in the part of the hospital that was destroyed. I'm afraid that is the last anyone remembers seeing them." Rosanna felt weak. She started to crumble to the ground. David caught her and she leaned against him. Before Rosanna had time to process what she had just heard, David quickly added, "But I do have some good news for you." She heard his voice but couldn't comprehend what he was telling her. The young man realized Rosanna was in a state of shock. His heart broke for what she was facing. For days she had been alone, surrounded by death and the unknown regarding her family. He gently led her through the crowd and pointed to a nearby bench. "There's some young ones who want to see you." Rosanna saw seated in a row, her children. She gave a quick, grateful glance at David, hardly believing her eyes.

She ran toward her children, "Oh dear God! Oh God!." The children ran into her arms, almost knocking her over. She then sank to her knees, touching each child, attempting to wipe away their tears while trying to hold back her own. She stared at each face, wanting to make sure this was not an illusion. Then she realized there were only three of them. The fourth child on the bench was a lost little boy searching for his family. She was overjoyed to see her children, hold them, but at the same time a part of her heart was breaking as she asked them, "Where's your little brother? Where's Albert?"

Roy started to cry. Junieta hesitated then said, "We don't know, Mama. The house was starting to shake and tilt. Mrs. Clarke took us out on the porch. She was holding Albert. A man came by and helped us. He came just in time, Mama. The house was turned upside down by the water and wind. He lifted Roy in his arms and told Elgiva and me to grab hold of his arms and not let go. Mrs. Clark and Albert were just behind us. Then they disappeared in the water. We haven't seen them since. Oh Mama!" Junieta buried her head in her mother's lap and sobbed.

Rosanna held her children tight and tried to comfort them. She had no words to say but rocked them all back and forth, Her eyes were dry, now, where just moments ago she had tried to hold back tears of joy. She stared into space. The pain went so deeply at the thought her little boy was gone, possibly forever. And she still hadn't found her baby girl. She was beyond tears. She silently spoke her thoughts to God. *'Is this the way it is? Have you taken two of my children to be with you? I prayed for their safety, but I meant on earth. If they're gone, I know they are safe with you. I know if they never come back to me, I know one day I will go to them. That's what The Psalm said, so I guess it's true for me?* Rosanna wasn't angry with God, but she was confused. She was numb. Her heart did cry out to Him, *Why? How can this be? I don't understand. I want them back in my arms.* She held tightly to the three children who had been spared. She never wanted to let go of them.

Chapter 17

I

For James and Earl it seemed like an eternity before they were finally allowed to go to the island. The father and son barely spoke to each other on the trip. Both were frozen with fear at what they might find. James had been checking the newspapers daily to see if any of his family's names were on the list of the dead. He knew the lists were incomplete, nor were they always accurate, but not finding their names posted gave him hope.

James and Earl tried to take as much food and clothes as they were allowed. They had heard and read reports of the devastation in Galveston; that the great majority of homes and buildings were totally destroyed, and whatever was left was badly damaged.

When they finally set foot on the island, they both felt they were in a strange land. Whatever they had heard or read did not prepare them for what they now saw with their own eyes. It was hard to get oriented since most of the landscape had been altered by the hurricane.

On inquiry they were told where they might find news of their family. They slowly made their way through the mountains of debris, piles being made as the city tried to clean up the horrendous mess. With handkerchiefs held to their noses, they tried to blot out the smell of the funeral pyres which burned day and night.

James felt sick at his stomach thinking Rosanna and the children had to face such a nightmare by themselves. He should have been here to protect them. But how was he to know this was going to happen! The forecast had said, 'tropical storm with rain and heavy winds'. The word hurricane was never used, at least when he and Earl left Galveston early that Saturday morning. He was grateful Earl had been spared this horrible ordeal. He wished his son could also be spared what he now saw.

James wasn't even sure they still had a family left. He had to find out one way or the other. The day was quickly coming to a close and he still hadn't reached the central location where he might find help in locating his family. They turned a corner and Earl saw Will Murney across the street.

"Will!" shouted Earl. Will squinted his eyes trying to see who had called his name. The growing darkness and crowds of people made it difficult to match the voice with a specific face.

In the meantime, Earl was waving his arms trying to get Will's attention. He made his way across the street as quickly as he could. James followed his son, not really sure what was happening. He knew Earl had recently made a friend, but had never met the boy. Once Earl came face to face with Will, he deliberately pulled back on his exuberance. He didn't want to embarrass his friend.

Short of breath, he said, "Hi, Will. This is my father," and nodded in the direction of James as he caught up to Earl.

"Glad to meet you, sir. Have you been on the island very long?" Will asked them, "I heard you went to the mainland that Saturday morning."

"We haven't been here long, actually, we just arrived this afternoon." James answered. "I've never seen anything like this. I can't take it in."

Will agreed. "I know. We're all in shock, sir."

Earl asked, "How's your brother?"

Will hesitated before answering. Bad news was always hard to tell. "Um, he didn't make it. All the kids in the orphanage drowned, except for me and two other guys. The nuns are gone, too. Nothing's left of the orphanage. What about your family?"

"Don't know yet. We're on our way to try to find them." Earl said.

"Well I won't hold you up. Good luck." Will said.

James and Earl thanked him and started again on their search. The seriousness of their search seemed heightened by the meeting with Will. Hearing that he had lost his brother, that he had no family left, made James think to himself, *At least Earl and I have each other if we find out we've lost the others.*

Night was approaching. Now the pyres helped light their way as they tried to reach their destination. The workers at the central information location were putting away their pens and files of gathered information, the stack growing daily. It was the end of a long day and time to leave. The phrase, 'go home' held no meaning for most of them.

James hurriedly approached the closest worker. Almost out of breath, he introduced himself, "Excuse me, ma'am. I'm James Steele and this is my son Earl. We just got to the island a little while ago. We've been stuck on the mainland because of the hurricane. Took a long time to get here. We're looking for my wife, Rosanna, and my five other children."

The woman looked at the man and saw the anxiousness in his face, an expression that was not exclusive to him. Something sounded familiar to her. "You said your name is Steele? I think I may have some information. Your name rings a bell." She lifted her lantern and brought it close to her box of papers. She flipped through two sections, finally stopping to pull out a page. "Yes, here is something." She looked up at James and smiled. James' heart skipped a beat with hope.

"Your family is staying in a section of the city where tents have been erected as temporary shelter. I can't draw you a map, but I can point you in the right direction. I don't think you'll have too much trouble finding the tents. People along the way can help you if needed. Turn around and go back east. You should find your family there. I have no idea which tent they're occupying but you'll find them." The woman said goodbye to the man and boy and said a silent prayer their search would be successful. She was Mrs. Parker, the same kind woman who had helped Rosanna days ago.

James and Earl were exhausted and now they were going to have to backtrack to find the tent housing. But there were no complaints from either one of them. They would walk to the ends of the earth to reach their family.

II

After three nights and two days, the two searchers finally found the community of tents.

"Papa, it looks like everyone is asleep. What do we do now?"

"Earl, it does seem like these people have settled in for the night. We shouldn't disturb them. I suggest we try to get some sleep. We've waited this long, I guess we can wait one more night."

They looked around and found an empty space where they could stretch out and get some rest.

"Papa," Earl said, "What can we do to not smell that awful stink?"

"Going to sleep is the only remedy I know of at the moment. Good night, son."

III

James was surprised when the sounds of the early morning risers woke him up. He wasn't surprised by the sounds as much as he was surprised he had fallen asleep. Last night he was restless, excited to see his family. He didn't think he could sleep at all knowing they were so near. It took every ounce of self-control to keep from barging in to each tent until he found Rosanna and the children.

He sat up and smoothed down his hair and brushed off his clothes. He felt the stubble on his chin and knew his mustache needed trimming, but he also knew his family wouldn't care about how he looked. He was now beyond being excited to find them. For days he didn't know if they were alive or injured or dead. He gently shook Earl to wake him up. He wanted both of them to be alert and begin searching the tents.

He started asking anyone who was up if they knew where to find the Steele family. On his fifth inquiry an elderly man pointed to the next to last tent at the end of the row. "I think it's that one."

James shook his hand and started to run towards the tent, then he stopped in his tracks, remembering he was leaving Earl behind. He turned and went back to his son. "We're doing this together."

They quietly entered the tent, hoping it was the right one. Pulling back the flap they let in the morning sun. He heard her voice before he saw her. It sounded frightened as she asked,

"Who's there? What do you want?"

Before she had time to say another word James was by her side, "It's me, Rosanna, and Earl is here with me. We've finally found you!"

Rosanna sat up, stunned to see her husband and son. She opened her eyes wide and shook her head side to side. "Is it really you? Looking around her husband's body to try to see Earl. She asked him, "Earl, are you alright?"

James then asked her, "How are you? That's what we want to know."

She couldn't answer him. She couldn't bear hearing herself tell him the news; at least not now. Let him have a few moments of happiness and joy in their reunion. That's what she was going to do, enjoy the moment for a little while.

"Earl, come closer. I want to see your face," Rosanna said, trying to avoid James' eyes and deliberately avoiding his question.

At this point the other children were starting to wake up. Roy was the first one to spot his father and brother. Almost as quick as lightening he threw himself on his Papa and gave a hug so tight it almost stopped James from breathing. The girls sat up, rubbing their eyes to make sure they were not dreaming.

"Papa, is that you, really you? Is that you Earl?" Elgiva asked.

Then Junieta started to cry tears of relief. Her Papa was here and everything was going to be better. "Oh, Papa'" she said as she hugged and showered him with kisses. Then she whispered in his ear, "Papa, I need to talk with you about Mama."

He nodded and said, "In a little while."

When the children calmed down, he helped Rosanna up from her cot and hugged her. He couldn't help but notice she had lost some weight in the short time they had been separated. He looked around the tent, expecting to see baby Mary bundled up, sleeping through all the excitement. He wondered where was Roy's shadow, little Albert? He gently loosened his hold on Rosanna and held her hands. He looked at her and tilted his head, "Rosanna." she knew what he was about to ask, but she started to answer his questions before he had a chance to open his mouth to speak.

Her words stuck in her throat, but she finally said, "The two little ones are not here. We're fairly sure they're gone. They didn't make it, James." There, she had told him the dreadful news. They were the crushing words no parent ever wanted to hear. Earl stood nearby, not believing what his mother was telling them; his family was the world to him.

There was no way to soften such a hard blow. The ringing of the breakfast bell was the only thing that briefly turned their attention from sorrow to the immediate needs of the children.

"We need to get breakfast for the children," Rosanna said. Neither she or James felt like eating. Earl didn't want any food. He suddenly didn't have an appetite.

"Son, you need to eat something. Got to keep up your strength," James told him. Earl obeyed, but without enthusiasm.

IV

After breakfast Junieta and Elgiva took their father by the hand and said, "Can we talk about Mama now? She's busy helping with the dishes."

James looked at his two daughters, amazed they had survived such an ordeal. It was miraculous for any healthy child to survive an experience like this storm, but these children were also battling Tuberculosis.

James had to ask them, "Won't your mother wonder where you are?"

"Oh no, she wants us to be with you. Papa, we're worried about Mama," Junieta said.

"It's true Papa, we are," added Elgiva.

"How so girls?"

"Mama hasn't cried at all since we found out about Albert and Mary. Doesn't she care about them? Didn't she love them? She doesn't seem sad they are gone."

"Now listen to me carefully, girls. I do not want you to worry about your mother. Of course she loved Albert and Mary; more than her own life. That's how she loves all her children. I've seen her shed enough tears in her lifetime to fill an ocean. But this time it's different. She's been hit so hard and her pain goes so deeply, she's afraid if she lets go of one tear, she won't be able to stop crying ever." James realized his words applied to him, also. He had adopted this way of coping with situations his whole life. He continued and tried to also impress on them, as young as they were, "And remember this, try not to measure someone else's grief by how many tears they shed. Every person deals with sadness in their own way. I know over time your mother will cry, but we may never see it. She wants to be strong for her family. Now don't get me wrong, crying is not a sign of weakness. It is good to cry. It sometimes helps us greatly, it helps us heal. So, don't think you're not strong if you do cry. Do you understand what I'm saying? I hope I haven't confused you."

"I think I understand, a little," said Junieta.

"I don't, but I'm still pretty young," offered Elgiva.

They were young, too young to have to go through such hard times, but James did resolve to talk with Rosanna. He wanted to make sure she knew he would never leave her alone again. He still felt guilty about not being with her through this tragedy.

V

It was several days before James had a chance to talk with Rosanna privately. They were both busy trying to help others find their way through homelessness and too often heartbreaking loneliness.

During one of those days, James had made his way to the part of the city where their home had once been. He searched around to see if there was anything worth salvaging. He was about to leave when something caught his eye. The sunlight reflected on a segment of glass. James bent down to see what was in the rubble. It was their small picture of the cottage that once hung on their parlor wall. The glass was shattered and the picture frame was cracked, but the picture was in remarkable condition. You could still read the poem on it.

A wave of anger swelled up inside him. He felt like tossing the picture, never wanting to see it again. Instead, he raised the picture to the sky and angrily shouted at God, "Is this some kind of joke?"

He waved the picture as if he was doing it in the very face of God. He continued his rant, "You save a two-bit picture, but don't save my precious children! It doesn't make sense. It's cruel!" Just as he was about to throw the picture as far as he could, something, a thought perhaps, perhaps an inner voice spoke to him.

In his hand he held the only thing, material, tangible thing from his home, that survived the horrific storm. It was a miracle in itself. Maybe God was telling him, *Wait a minute.* Then, James stopped. *What am I doing talking to God? I don't even know if he exists.* His mind wouldn't stop. He kept thinking, maybe God was telling him, " If I can save a two-bit picture, I can do other unimaginable things." James lowered his head, still angry God didn't save his Albert and Mary and the other thousands who perished that terrible night on September 8, 1900.

He then turned and made his way back to Rosanna and the children; the picture firmly held in his hand.

VI

James showed Rosanna what he had found that morning. She took the picture and held it to her heart. Her face softened as she said, "Remember, this was one of the gifts Mama gave me right before she died. She told me she wanted me to have it always and hoped that I could hang it in my home as she happily had done in her's years ago. I feel like I still have a part of her with me. I can't believe you found it. This whole city has been turned upside down. Thank you so much for finding it and bringing it to me." She gave James a kiss of gratitude on his cheek. He was so glad he hadn't thrown it away. He thought this might be a good time to talk with Rosanna, try to find out how she was really doing. Just as he started to talk with her, the children came up to them, wanting some attention. James would have to wait until later that night, when the children were asleep.

It was another two nights before James had an opportunity to speak with Rosanna. The children were sound asleep on their pallets. Rosanna was busy braiding her hair as she had done a thousand times over the years of their marriage. James looked at her and wondered how she could be so strong facing all the trials they had experienced in the past and now, the hardest one of all. He could not understand this strength that seemed to radiate from deep inside her; or perhaps she was in some kind of strange denial.

"Rosanna, you puzzle me beyond my scope of understanding how you cannot blame your God for this horrendous loss. We've lost everything; home, clothing and most tragically, two of our children. What kind of God allows such things to happen?

Rosanna took hold of her husband's hands and looked into his steely gray eyes. "Why do you call Him, 'my God'?"

James then confessed, "I've seen you reading the Bible late at night. I wasn't spying on you. It was very late one night and you hadn't come to bed. I was worried about you. I got up to check on you and saw you reading. You seemed so absorbed I didn't want to interrupt you so I went back to bed. Why did you hide your reading from me?"

Rosanna was so surprised at the direction this conversation was taking. She thought he had wanted to talk with her about their future. Well, here it was, he was asking her about God. "I know your opinion of religion and didn't want to upset you. Look at you now. You're angry at a God you don't even know. And I don't have an answer for your question as how God could let something like this happen.

"God never guaranteed any human being, except for the very first man and woman in the Garden of Eden, in the beginning of time, that life would be perfect; that there would not be troubles to face and sorrows to bear. He promised them a life of no pain, no disease, no struggles of any kind in life. Everything was perfect for them, but they threw it away, James. They fell for a lie from Satan himself. God didn't cause all this pain and suffering. They did. And one more thing James, this is what I know in my heart; I am sure our little ones are with Him now. And I believe they were personally escorted to heaven by two 'angels' on this earth, Molly and her mother. I look around us James and I too, am broken hearted to see the devastating destruction, the loss of life. You are wrong, though. We have not lost everything. We have each other and four of our children. I have heard of families who lost all their children. Mr. Cline, the meteorologist lost his wife and the child she was carrying. Mr. Benson lost his wife and all his children. I could go on and on. The question, 'Why' may be with us forever. I can only trust there was a reason this happened to us and others. I know there's an emptiness in my heart that will never go away. I'll always long to see and hold our little ones. I know you feel that way, too. We can only ask God to help us get through this, though I know we'll never get over it." Her eyes never let go of his face.

James had nothing else to say. It had been years since he had heard that much 'Bible talk' and certainly hadn't expected a sermon from his wife. He sat there in silence. He envied his wife's strength and calm through such a time as this and was surprised he didn't resent her strange words. He took her in his arms and for the first time in their marriage, tears swelled in his eyes. He slowly let go a few tears, struggling to control them. *Rosanna was right,* he told himself, I *don't know her God. Maybe It is time I should get to know him. He must be real, for if it wasn't for God,* James continued to tell himself, *I know my wife well enough to know she would never be able to endure such a loss as this without her God.*

Feeling the strength of her husband's arms around her, Rosanna clung to him and laid her head on his chest. Tears started to roll down her cheeks, the first tears she had shed since the awful night of the storm. She was no longer beyond tears.

Epilogue

The Galveston Island went through a long, but successful rebirth. It is still not known an exact count of how many perished on Saturday, September 8, 1900. It is estimated 6,000 to 8,000 people died on the Island. That number does not include surrounding areas that were affected by the storm nor does it include casualties from a string of tornadoes that were born from the hurricane.

Many residents stayed to help rebuild the island. James and Rosanna Steele decided it was best for them to leave Galveston and start a new life with their four surviving children. The health of Junieta and Elgiva were their primary reason for leaving. It was too much of a risk having them exposed to the unsanitary conditions the city suffered after the storm. Fighting the spread of disease was one of many battles that had to be fought after the devastation and tremendous loss of life.

It is recorded in the 1910 census that the Steele family lived in Dallas, Texas. In 1912 on February 8, Junieta lost her battle with Tuberculosis. She was twenty-two years old. Their next move was to New Mexico, still searching for a healthy environment for Elgiva. It is recorded that on December 19, 1927 Elgiva passed away in Truth or Consequences, New Mexico. She was thirty-five years old. James and Rosanna moved to Crowell, Texas to join Earl and Roy, who now had families of their own.

James and Rosanna lived the remainder of their life in Crowell, Texas. On July 21, 1943, at the age of eighty-six, James passed away. Four years later, on May 24, 1947, Rosanna passed away. She was eighty-four years old.

Earl married Edna Shelton, his first wife. They had ten children; two daughters and eight sons. Earl lived to be eighty-five years old. He passed away on July 20, 1973.

Roy married Jesse Lee Cates and had one son who they lost in World War II.

Roy was married three times and a widower three times.

Albert and baby Mary were recorded among the thousands who perished in the Great Storm of Galveston, Texas on September 8, 1900.

James and Rosanna out lived four of their children. God blessed them with eleven grandchildren. My husband, George G. Steele II was the son of George G. Steele, Sr and Lil Steele; grandson of Earl and Edna Steele. I had the privilege of knowing both Earl and Roy Steele. They never spoke of their experience and survival of the 1900 Galveston Hurricane in my presence. It was in later years that different family members told me of the family's ordeals and tragedies; Earl's birth defect and subsequent surgeries, Junieta and Elgiva's battle with Tuberculosis, and that Albert and Mary died in the hurricane. Many references to the Steele family in the story are based on true events. Much of their story is entirely from my imagination. There are other characters in the book that are based on true people and events; The Cline brothers, Isaac and Joseph, Isaac's wife, Cora May and their three children, Will Murney and the mention of his brother, the tragedy of the orphanage and the children and nuns who perished in the storm. The letter, written by Molly in the story, was an actual letter written during the storm, the author unknown. I chose Molly to be the author of the letter in an attempt to give a name and a face to such a touching appeal for help. We know it was written by a young woman, deeply in love, and desperately hoping to be rescued. Her letter survived. There is no evidence that she survived.

The hymn, "What a Friend We Have in Jesus" was written by Joseph M. Scriven 1855, a poem written for his mother. It was put to music in 1866 by Charles C. Converse.

All other characters in the story are fiction. Great effort was used in attempting to be historically accurate when referring to the storm and the after effects. Any departure from accuracy is due to human error and not intentional. The main goal of telling the story of James and Rosanna Steele is to relate their courage and perseverance through extremely difficult times. It is about two people who loved each other, stayed together and "for richer, for poorer; in sickness and in health, 'til death do us part.' fulfilled their vows.

In the seventh grade I chose to write a report on the Galveston Hurricane of 1900, mainly because of my fondness for the island, born from having precious family members who took my sisters and I to the island several times during summer vacations. Since then I have had a keen interest in that period of Texas history. It was not a morbid interest in the worst natural disaster to ever hit the United States of America in loss of life, but the story of the courage and determination of the people who rebuilt the city and made it safer by building a sea wall seventeen feet higher than the beach. They also added huge granite boulders to re-enforce the strength of the wall. The city raised over two thousand buildings, ensuring the city's highest point was well over eight feet above sea level. It was a remarkable work of engineering. There were many who left the city, never wanting to see it again for understandable reasons and I have no criticism of them at all. They had their reasons, as did the James Steele family had their's. I cannot imagine experiencing the nightmare that occurred that September night. I may have wanted to stay and help the people to recover and rebuild their homes. I possibly would have walked away and never wanted to see the Gulf again. Who can say unless we were there, but we were not. It was over a hundred years ago.

Acknowledgements

I greatly appreciate the help I obtained from my father-in-law, George G. Steele Sr, who patiently answered my questions about his family, and any memories he had of his father, Earl, his Uncle Roy, and grandparents, James and Rosanna.

When faced with challenges in technology, I am especially indebted to my grandchildren and daughter-in-law, Lisa. I am blessed to have grandchildren, children and their spouses, sisters, and friends who sweetly listened to my ideas about the story and encouraged me to write this book.

It is with heartfelt gratefulness that I want to thank my daughter, Emily and her best friend, Charisse (like a daughter to me) for spending time reading and editing the manuscript.

The help I received from the people at the Rosenberg Library is also greatly appreciated. If you, the reader, get a chance to visit Galveston, I highly recommend a visit to the Rosenberg Library. They have meticulously preserved documents and artifacts, which miraculously survived, the Galveston Hurricane of 1900.

Suggested Reading

Isaac's Storm: A Man, a Time, and the Deadliest Hurricane in History
   By Erik Larson
   Published 1999

Storms, Floods and Sunshine: A Book of Memoirs
   By Isaac Cline
   Originally Published 1945

Through a Night of Horrors: Voices From the 1900 Galveston Storm
   Edited by Casey Edward Green and Shelly Henley Kelly

"The Forgotten Epidemic", a documentary on the Tuberculosis Disease

9 781546 270706